SWING LOW

SWING LOW

—

BLACK MEN WRITING

—

by

REBECCA CARROLL

Introduction by

CLAUDE BROWN

CAROL SOUTHERN BOOKS
NEW YORK

—

PHOTOGRAPH CREDITS:

David Bradley: copyright © 1994 by Carole Patterson
Cecil Brown: Randi Rucker
Wesley Brown: Jacqui Castro
Cornelius Eady: Lois Bernstein
Trey Ellis: Lara Belmonte
Leon Forrest: Karen L. Blackwell
Henry Louis Gates, Jr.: Sarah Putnam
Charles Johnson: Jerry Bauer
Yusef Komunyakaa: Mandy Sayer
Nathan McCall: Catherine Pugh
Caryl Phillips: Jillian Edelstein
Darryl Pinckney: Dominique Nabokov
Ishmael Reed: Jerry Bauer
Greg Tate: Dawoud Bey
John Edgar Wideman: News Office, Univ. of Mass., Amherst
August Wilson: Cori Wells Braun

Published by Carol Southern Books in hardcover and by Crown Trade Paperbacks, both imprints of Crown Publishers, Inc., 201 East 50th Street, New York, New York 10022. Member of the Crown Publishing Group.

Random House, Inc.   New York, Toronto, London, Sydney, Auckland

Carol Southern Books and colophon and Crown Trade Paperbacks and colophon are trademarks of Crown Publishers, Inc.

Manufactured in the United States of America.

Library of Congress Cataloging-in-Publication Data
Swing low: Black men writing / [compiled by] Rebecca Carroll. — 1st ed.
     p.   cm.
   1. American literature—Afro-American authors—History and criticism—Theory, etc.
2. American literature—20th century—History and criticism—Theory, etc.   3. American literature—Men authors—History and criticism—Theory, etc.   4. Afro-American authors—20th century—Interviews.   5. Afro-American men—Intellectual life.   6. Afro-American men in literature.   7. Afro-Americans in literature.   I. Carroll, Rebecca.
PS153.N5S94   1995
810.9'896073—dc20
                                                                              94-33373
                                                                              CIP

ISBN 0-517-59981-3
ISBN 0-517-88324-4 Pbk.
10 9 8 7 6 5 4 3 2 1
First Edition

For
my two younger brothers,
Pepe and Kiko Lopez Waldron

ACKNOWLEDGMENTS

I'd like to swing thanks, as well as deep love and appreciation, to the following people for their encouragement, safe refuge, and for their faith in my vision—my parents, David and Laurette Carroll; Mother Jan, Monique Cormier and Tom Palladino, Carmen Grau, Thomas Hills, Caryn Rivers, Shelby Gaines, Skip Gates, Peter Glenshaw, Sherry Lovelace, the Department of Afro-American Studies at Harvard University; my agent, Meredith Bernstein; my publisher, Carol Southern; my tremendously patient editor, Eliza Scott; and to Matty, for supplying the oxygen when I needed to breathe deep.

To the writers in *Swing Low*—
I have learned how to crawl, walk, and sing through the deep hush and the slow, sweet rhythm of our history as black people. The writers in this book have guided my journey, mentored my notes, and offered their own voices as unfeigned testimony of what lies ahead and behind. Their voices are strong and resonant, thick and deep, similar to those voices that sang and kept faith with the gospel: "Swing Low, Sweet Chariot, Coming for to carry me home. . . ." In various and mesmerizing hymns, single words, and colorful phrases, the writers in this book have created a gospel . . . about writing, about language, and about being black. My most sincere and heartfelt gratitude to the sixteen writers in this volume, who believed in this book and who followed through on that belief.

This book remembers and celebrates the voice of Ralph Ellison, whose enlightened and divine commitment to the written word acted as the sweet chariot that may well have come for to carry all of us home.
—Rebecca Carroll, April 1994

CONTENTS

INTRODUCTION
  BY CLAUDE BROWN   ix

DAVID BRADLEY   1

CECIL BROWN   20

WESLEY BROWN   36

CORNELIUS EADY   53

TREY ELLIS   67

LEON FORREST   82

HENRY LOUIS GATES, JR.   98

CHARLES JOHNSON   113

YUSEF KOMUNYAKAA   128

NATHAN McCALL   141

CARYL PHILLIPS   161

DARRYL PINCKNEY   177

ISHMAEL REED   191

GREG TATE   206

JOHN EDGAR WIDEMAN   223

AUGUST WILSON   245

INTRODUCTION
by Claude Brown

At the 1956 Newport Jazz Festival, Paul Gonzalves, a tenor saxophonist in Duke Ellington's band, played twenty-eight soul-stirring choruses of "Diminuendo and Crescendo in Blue," each chorus achieving a greater intensity of spiritual arousal than the preceding one, provoking a significant, and rapidly expanding, segment of the audience to participate in what the city fathers misconstrued as mass hysteria. Normally staid, reserved, proper, and painfully well-bred debutantes and Ivy Leaguers, to the utter mortification of their parents, were not only being seduced by the Pied Piper music of Gonzalves into a dancing frenzy, but they were also tearing their clothes off and discarding their Bergdorf, Saks, and Bonwit Teller undergarments all over the place, with total abandon.

Needless to say, this was an extremely distressing scene for the old monied paragons of conservatism who formed the pillars of that sedate community of social dinosaurs.

A highly contagious "aesthetic seizure" or an "artistic fit" is how I choose to label the phenomenon of Paul Gonzalves's blowing those ever crescending choruses and the audience's response to his profoundly inspired soulful performance. Most of us who grew up black anywhere the African diaspora touched soil, North America, South America, the Caribbean, have seen and/or heard an aesthetic seizure and reacted to it in whatever way was natural for the individual. African-Americans are stimulated to dance in response to certain irresistible rhythms; we are incited to shouting our approval of exceptional oratory. With very few exceptions the greatest black orators of the twentieth century were products of the black Baptist church: Benjamin Mays, Mordecai Johnson,

Howard Thurmond, Martin Luther King, Jr., Gardner C. Taylor, Samuel Proctor, Thomas Kilgore Jr., Frederick Sampson, to name a few. It is irrefutable that oratory's spiritual potency is as equally spellbinding and soul stirring as music, dance, painting, and writing.

A common creative trait shared by an enormous preponderance of African-American artists, especially musicians, orators, and writers, is an individual need for varying lengths of warm-up time on the "ax"; in the pulpit; at the computer or word processor before they commence to "cook." The rare exceptions to this rule are genuine geniuses whose gifts are most easily recognized among performing artists such as musicians, singers, and dancers. Charlie Parker, John Coltrane, Miles Davis, Sarah Vaughn, and Judith Jamison are among the anointed few who possessed the capacity to instantly experience an infinitely infectious aesthetic seizure.

Normally, writing, which I consider to be an affliction rather than a hallowed gift, requires a lengthier warm-up period than most other arts. Only writers speak of sitting at their typewriters or various other instruments for the better part of an hour or more in persistent pursuit of the tenaciously elusive muse. Occasionally, the artistic seizure is achieved so quickly, with the words flowing so rapidly and eloquently, that the sense of elation or rapture is unnoticed until it subsides. Unglorified, writing is a burdensome, agonizing, perilous intellectual malady.

In 1975, I had a fortuitous encounter with a dear friend who I had not seen or spoken to for several years—Cecil Brown. Replying to my question about what significant changes had occurred in his life since we last spoke, Cecil informed me that he recently returned from Mexico, where he was working on a film with Warren Beatty. My surprised and puzzled reaction was verbalized in the statement: "Cecil, you're a writer, not a filmmaker." "No man, not anymore. I realized I'm too gregarious to be a writer." "You care to elaborate on that cryptic declaration?" "Claude, as a profession, writing is too lonely for me. So I decided to go into a collaborative occupation where I could work with people and minimize my loneliness."

Cecil's explanation was more perplexing than his initial response, prompting more questions: Was he unaware of how relentlessly possessive the art of writing is, and that desertion and abandonment are practical impossibilities? Contrarily, whoever heard of a writer interpreting solitude as anything worse than consecrated seclusion? Perhaps Cecil—as many naive scribes—was entertaining the delusion that he had elected to become a writer, in lieu of having been selected by destiny?

Recently history suggests that in due course Cecil discovered that for writers, abstention from writing creates the most profoundly painful loneliness imaginable, evolving into an utterly immobilizing and mentally crippling ennui. There exists a solitary cure for this anguished malaise; it is not sex, liquor, or drugs. Writing, and solely writing, is the miracle remedy.

In this collection of interviews—which reads more like an anthology—with a highly diversified sampling of some of America's truly talented and accomplished, current and future literary luminaries, the reader is treated to a fascinating, eloquent, and lucid exposition of the literary creative process and the cultural, historical, and social conditions responsible for creating these exceptionally gifted artists.

Each interviewee clearly describes how the African-American experience impacted upon him as an individual, an artist, and primarily as a writer, an African-American writer. This compendium of interviews constitutes a candid, unadulterated cultural representation of a substantial spectrum of the African-American experience resulting in a concourse of extraordinarily talented scribes for the intellectual enrichment of the entire global literati.

The size of this tome is deceptive. What appears to be an opuscule at first glance, is actually a magnum opus in disguise. It is replete with an awesome opulence of erstwhile undisclosed information pertaining to the development of, and functioning as, a male African-American writer in a white male-dominated society. This unique compilation abounds with resounding echoes of a specific literary ancestry including such historical notables as Countee Cullen, Langston Hughes, Chester Himes, Richard Wright, Ralph Ellison, James Baldwin, etc.—writers who speak directly to their cultural descendants in terms, descriptions, images, and voices we immediately understand and cherish as a precious heritage.

From William Welles Brown to Wesley Brown, the African-American wordsmiths have been immensely enhancing the canon of American literature as no other group of Americans—having been spared the black American experience—is qualified to do.

The forefathers of this nation nuked the souls of our ancestors just as surely as if an atom bomb had been dropped onto the spiritual soil or genes of our progenitors and rendered that soil incapable of producing normal, mentally healthy progeny—or any progeny at all. The social nuclear bomb was the establishment of the African slave trade and horrors of the Middle Passage. Nagasaki and Hiroshima are metaphors for slavery and the ensuing years of lynchings and other racist atrocities inflicted on succeeding generations of African-Americans.

It is equally unpredictable to state when, or if, African-Americans will fully recover from the culturally and psychologically mutilating effects of slavery and practically 130 years of vicious and ruthless racism, as it is to prognosticate when, or if, the victims of Hiroshima and Nagasaki will ever be the foreparents of a genetically and anatomically salubrious generation; or if the land within a twenty-five-mile radius of the bomb's direct impact will ever again spawn vegetation.

There exists no artistic medium more appropriate for describing in minute, graphic, sensuous, anguished, and jubilant detail the African-American saga than the various forms of literature. The scribes contributing to this collection have very eloquently imparted the agony, humiliation, death, and death-defying suffering, mentally and emotionally crippling injuries, and the ecstasy of sensing the indomitability of the human spirit that enabled the African-American to survive the American ordeal with his soul intact and to flourish in spite of it.

Yusef Komunyakaa, who writes to define himself, provocatively expounds on the metaphysics of writing. *David Bradley's* comparison of Nathan McCall's writing to that of Susan Brownmiller is so confounding it is virtually mind boggling. Upon reading that jolting line, I instantly felt an irresistible urge to reread all of Susan Brownmiller's work. Apparently, I have grossly misconstrued her writing. And the fact that *Nathan McCall* devotes seventy-five percent of his interview to apologizing to African-American women for having revealed more truth in his autobiography than they can tolerate should prove to be extremely instructive to aspiring writers contemplating producing autobiographies.

Greg Tate, whose novel-in-progress I eagerly await, is doing something excitingly different, which will undoubtedly become one of the most valuable additions to African-American literature and American literature in this decade. And *Ishmael Reed*, who is never less than interesting and unintentionally entertaining, exhibits vintage Ishmael Reed. His interview is the most instantly riveting of the lot. How can any reader avoid enthusiastically turning the pages of an interview, essay, article, novel, etc., that begins with the subject essentially announcing that "I am a bad nigger from a family of bad niggers. We all carry weapons and my weapon is the most lethal of them all—the written word."

Only *John Edgar Wideman* voices an appreciation of the proposition that writing is a serious affliction symptomized by alternating seizures of insecurity and egotism. And *August Wilson's* interview irrefutably confirms the notion that, with negligibly few exceptions, African-American male writers arrive at their professional destinies via the same or a similar path: the commonality of culture and experiences that are virtually inevitable when growing up black and male in America. The black man's social and cultural legacy in this nation has uniquely qualified him to poignantly write of Nat Turner's rage, after going sane and slaying his oppressors, and the emasculated, servile character of Miss Daisy's chauffeur with equally compelling credibility.

From William Welles Brown to Wesley Brown, we have, each and all, paid our dues to the muse by laboring exhaustively and persistently in the vineyards of literary creativity; having done so, we will never again be intimidated by that most terrifying of monsters—a blank sheet of paper glaring menacingly at us from a silent typewriter.

This book is fated to become a literary collectible and it deserves nothing less, for it is truly a treasure.

All you are ever told about being black is that it is a terrible, terrible thing to be. Now, in order to survive this, you have to dig down into yourself and re-create yourself, really, according to no image which yet exists in America. You have to impose, in fact—this may sound strange—you have to decide who you are, and force the world to deal with you, not with its idea of you.

—James Baldwin

All Inside My Soul
Black Poet's First Poem

When they call me nigger
Ra awakens
Osiris cries
Isis screams
Ramsies' armies
rage up sand storms
from stolen graves
the great stone Zimbabwe
squeezes milk curdled from
    pain
Shaka Zulu screams across the
    plains
The Atlantic whispers
creaks of rotten wood
and tattered sails

the holding pen
walls of Senegal's Gore
Island crumble
eroded by malice
Patrice Lamumba and Samora
    Michelle
drop hand grenades into
    myself
and nod when the shrapnel
tears my tissue
when they call me nigger
Set sails
and history wails
All Inside my Soul.

—Michael C. Ladd

DAVID BRADLEY

DAVID BRADLEY is a graduate of the University of Pennsylvania (B.A., 1972) and the Institute of United States Studies, the University of London (M.A., 1974). He is the author of two novels, *South Street* (1975) and *The Chaneysville Incident* (1981), and numerous reviews and essays that have been published in such periodicals as *Esquire, Redbook, The Nation, The New York Times Magazine*, and *The Pennsylvania Gazette*. He won the PEN/Faulkner Award and was nominated for the National Book Award for *The Chaneysville Incident*. Bradley has been a National Achievement Scholar, a Presidential Scholar, a Thouron British-American Exchange Scholar, and a recipient of fellowships from the John Simon Guggenheim Foundation and the National Endowment for the Arts. He has been a visiting professor at Colgate University, the University of California, San Diego, and the Massachusetts Institute of Technology and has been a permanent faculty member at Temple University in Philadelphia since 1976, where he is currently professor of English.

W RITING IS NATURAL. You tell stories, you write them down.

I grew up in the church. My religion is African Methodist Episcopal Zion, which is basically Methodist. My great-grandfather was a slave who purchased his own freedom, after which he became a minister in the AME Zion church. My grandfather, my grand uncle, and my father were all AME Zion ministers straight down the line. Our life was about the church, so any forms of expression we chose would be expressed through the church. Music, words, rhythm, passion—all of those things that one might find in a church were an important part of my life growing up. I hated the finger exercises that I had to do in order to play an instrument, so I sang in the choir all the way through college. I didn't quit the glee club until after my junior year, which is about the time I started writing my first novel, *South Street*. That is what we did in the church—we expressed ourselves; I preached sermons, sang hymns, and told stories. When I first got to college, and read Emily Dickinson, I found the rhythm of her poetry to be similar to that of the hymns I had grown up hearing every Sunday morning in church. Since I had not read much poetry growing up, nor very much literature, the connection I could make between the Sunday morning hymns and the rhythm of Dickinson's poetry made it easier to read and understand other literature as well.

I have never had much visual talent and was deeply disturbed when I discovered that you can *learn* how to draw. So I always chose forms of expressions that came naturally to me, that I knew I had a talent for. Certainly there is visualization in writing, but it does not require hand-eye coordination, which I don't have. I came from a town called Bedford, which is about two hundred miles west of Philadelphia. When I was a kid, there were maybe fifty blacks in Bedford. There were five traffic lights in this town, and there still are five traffic lights. I came to Philadelphia to go to college. The first night I got here, I looked out the window of my room and saw a street with more traffic lights lined up in a row than there were combined in my entire hometown. So I became curious. I started walking down that street. It's a strange street, Spruce Street. It runs from the University of Pennsylvania freshman dormitories all the way down across the Schuylkill and then becomes South Street on the other side. In fact, right in the middle of the river it becomes South Street because the bridge over the river is called the South Street Bridge. Spruce Street continues on again about three or four blocks east, which is a very affluent part of Center City, Philadelphia. South Street borders the South Philadelphia ghetto.

The ghetto was something that I knew nothing about. I wasn't afraid of it because the people in it turned out to be just like the people who I grew up with, except they drank a lot more. I spent time there because I felt that it provided me with the sense of a small-town black community at a time when I was thrust into a city and a white university. Although I grew up in a white town, I had never been surrounded by predominantly Eurocentric, white culture. The University of Pennsylvania was elite, Jewish, white, academic—which was fascinating but was also suffocating.

John Edgar Wideman was my advisor at Penn. He directed my degree because there was no creative writing department. So periodically I would go in to see him and show him my course registration form and tell him what I was doing, and he would say it was fine, and that was really the extent of our relationship. He was my first creative writing teacher, but we had this sort of weird, dancey relationship, as most black people did in academic institutions at that time. You know how when white people see too many black people getting too tight they start worrying. John was a big deal in the administration; at one point he was the director of Black Studies. He was at a different level. He was a college professor. When I went to college, being a college professor was neither understood nor traditionally valued by most black people, because it meant that you had sold out. The sellout concept was a new one for me because I didn't realize that anyone was buying!

I wasn't particularly interested in finding a mentor, so that type of relationship was never created between John and I. He was doing his thing, and I was doing mine. Both of us were from western Pennsylvania, though, and we had a lot of funny stuff in common, like having had the same Sunday school teacher. She had moved from Pittsburgh, where John is from, to Bedford, where I am from, and into a little house down the street, or down the field rather (we didn't have streets), from our house. And then, of course, we both experienced the bombing of MOVE, which John would later write about in his novel *Philadelphia Fire*.

I have lived off and on in Philadelphia for twenty-five years. There hasn't been a six-month period during those twenty-five years when I have been away from this city. I have taught at Temple University for eighteen years. I am familiar with Philadelphia. When the bombing of MOVE happened, I was at my mother's, because I remember that it was Mother's Day. In its simplest form, there was a group of black people called MOVE, who were known as a "back to nature" group. In reality, they were a bunch of schizophrenic crazy people; a cult. When the group started back in the seventies they did a lot of very good things. They were able to help many people get off drugs and move on with their lives and that sort of thing, but over the years the group sort of lost its way. By the time the bombing occurred, the group was living in a house in West Philadelphia that the members had appropriated, and they were terrorizing the neighborhood.

When I say "back to nature," I mean *nature;* they didn't bathe, they didn't change their clothes, they were leaving food outside for the maggots, feeding the cockroaches, and haranguing the neighborhood with a bullhorn at all hours of the day. A few years before, there had been a confrontation between MOVE and the police in which an officer had died. Apparently the police had shot the officer by accident, but it was blamed on MOVE. MOVE had gotten so out of control by that time that they were entrapped by the FBI for allegedly attempting to purchase an atomic bomb. Why they would want to buy an atomic bomb, no one knows. At any rate, the city responded to all of this life-threatening chaos in an inappropriate way and eventually dropped a bomb on the MOVE house, which ended up burning down the entire block.

It was a very traumatic time because all of us outside of the whole operation were scared out of our minds. We had no idea what was going on. There is a phenomenon here in Philadelphia that happens when the city burns off excess gases down at the refinery south of town—the sky kind of lights up. Well, the city was burning up gases the night they dropped the bomb, so we all thought the whole city was on fire. Wilson Goode, the city's first black mayor, was down at the art museum sipping white wine while the cops were borrowing helicopters from the state police so that they could drop this bomb. The mayor never dealt with it. It was embarrassing, stupid, ridiculous. It became convoluted, and fatal.

At the end of the day, what it was was a bunch of guys fucking up. It was not the beginning of the sixties all over again—MOVE people were not worthy of the spirited defense and the ideological integrity of the sixties movement. MOVE had no ideology. Each member would claim to be only one year in age and existence, and they all took the last name Africa. But they were part of our city, and the city dropped the bomb, and people died, so it became an historical event. I was never interested in writing about it because I felt that it was a city-shared experience—I didn't feel the need to reinvent it. Also, I was busy writing about other things at the time.

There are things in my life that I can think about stopping, but writing isn't one of them. It's like breathing—it's what I do. I don't even consider what I will write next, how long it will be, or when it will be finished—writing is ongoing and continuous for me. I like how writing allows me to lose time. As several editors right now will tell you, when I sit down to write, I sit for a long time and write for even longer. I can look at the clock before I start writing, and the next time I look up three hours will have passed. Usually the reason for my work going in late to editors is not because I'm not working on it, but because I am. I overwrite everything. I like finding things out. I like putting things together. I like words. There's nothing about writing that I don't like.

The only way I know that I have overwritten something is if I get an assignment for three thousand words and realize midway through the assignment that I have written forty thousand words. The only way to make something simple is to understand it in a very complicated way; to understand all of the complexities and ironies, and then to smooth out the bumps. I have a friend who is a great journalist—he doesn't even see the complexities, he just goes until he gets three thousand clean words. I can't write that way. I write because I want to understand things, I want to understand people, and I want to see how things might work out even if it is only in my head. And that takes some time. To do what is wanted, to do what is efficient, to do what is sensible—essentially just to do the job of writing—is of absolutely no interest to me. I don't care how much it pays. If I'm going to write, I'm going to *write*.

I started teaching at Temple for a lot of reasons, but mainly as a way of smoothing out the financial bumps of, say, buying a house. I always thought that as soon as I finished writing *The Chaneysville Incident* I would be a writer, and that's it. I was about thirty at that time, and I discovered that there were things that I wanted, and that my interactions with society would be made much simpler if I had a job. You can't get a mortgage if you walk into a bank and say, "I'm a freelance writer, last year I made $30,000, this year I might make $2,000." I had to make a decision about what kind of battles I wanted to fight. I decided that I would much rather fight with paper and word processors than have to worry about the check.

To be a writer full-time is also to be very lonely. I have certainly learned a lot from interacting with my students. Before I started teaching, I worked in publishing. I read the slush pile—all the unsolicited manuscripts. In the two and a half years that I did that as a job, I saw a million mistakes that I swear I will never make. I learned a lot about writing at that job, as dismal and monotonous as it was. Usually writers have to make their own mistakes, but when you sit at a job like that—nine to five, reading x number of manuscripts a week and then writing a report about them—you lose your tolerance for certain artistic excesses, and all the manuscripts become uninteresting and irresponsible writing. What is wonderful about teaching is that I get to work with my students on those same sorts of mistakes, instead of just cringing at them and filing a report at the end of the week.

I try not to let any of my writing go until I am at least marginally satisfied with it. If I don't want to read it, I don't think anybody else should have to. I am working on a piece for *The New*

York Times right now that I don't like. I don't like the assignment, I think it's a dumb idea—but it was in demand, so I agreed to do it, and I shouldn't have, but I did, so now I have to work on it until I find something in it that I like. I've been chipping away at it for a long time, but so far I haven't been able to carve anything that I think is worth paying attention to.

The assignment is to write an article about a bunch of books by black men in America—not about the "plight of black men," but about the books about the "plight of black men"—some that are by the black men who are plighting, and some from black men who haven't plighted at all. I think I picked the wrong conceit. I picked Frederick Douglass, who interests me, when I probably should have picked Bigger Thomas, who doesn't interest me. There is an awful way in which we all want the anger of Bigger, rather than the righteousness of Frederick. I'll probably end up throwing away the first part and rewriting it based on this tendency of society to look at Bigger Thomas as the representative for the black man in America.

This predisposition is a conflict for me because as a middle-aged, fairly affluent black man, I am painfully aware that I have never had, nor have I ever particularly desired, a classic ghetto experience. When I went to Penn, during the fifties, there was no slack for black people. We weren't supposed to be in the white academic world at all. By the late sixties, there were a couple of slots for black people that were acceptable; one was the northern urban black ghetto, and the other was southern rural. I was northern rural. So even when the slots were made and the roles were acceptable, I didn't fit. I wasn't a Baptist, I was a Methodist. I knew all about cows, chickens, and all that country stuff. I had never seen a rat or a cockroach until I moved to the city. So when I try to understand what young black men are going through now, and what young men say they are going through—in some senses I have to take their word for it. It's not that I don't see what is going on, but I can't relate to some of the more prominent young black voices, like Nathan McCall and Brent Staples, who are talking about the mind-set of the black man, and how the black man deals with his place in society.

When I read books like *Makes Me Wanna Holler*, things in the narrative start to sing not of authenticity, but of sociology. There are parts of Nathan McCall's book that sound like they came straight out of Susan Brownmiller. I don't believe him. And maybe I should believe him—I'm not the voice from the ghetto that can disprove anything Nathan McCall is saying. Of course, Nathan McCall isn't a voice from the ghetto either, when you get right down to it. If some young black men are saying that the only way they can feel strong is with a gun, I'm not going to be the person to say that they shouldn't try to feel strong. But do they *really* feel strong? My bullshit detector is sort of trembling, but it's not going off. If these men really do feel this way about guns and violence—what can we do to change it? I have found myself thinking these horribly middle-class and conventional things, like church and segregation.

When I was on South Street twenty-five years ago, I felt I understood the motivations of the people because I had seen people I grew up with acting the same way and doing the same kinds of things. I felt that they knew where their lives were not going to go but were determined to try and go there anyway, which was not what sociology said they should do. I could understand that they were fighting like hell. I want to tell some of these young black men today that I really don't understand how they think that killing other black people helps them to deal with the way that the white man has done them wrong. I don't understand how they could possibly believe that shit. I've read enough and seen enough to know that to most young black men today, putting down another brother, raping a sister, and using a gun somehow seem to be an attack on the outside world. And I don't believe that any of that is any more than a put-down brother, a raped sister, and another dead person.

Self-defense, fine. Fear and self-awareness, fine. Undirected anger, fine. *Inarticulate* anger, fine. But we are talking now about young black men who are supposed to be able to articulate that anger, which means that at some point they should be able to say more than "The TV made me do it." I don't have the answer, and I'm not sure that I need to have one to write this piece I am working on. I understand that conditions exist, but I don't think you have to kill your brothers, and I don't think you have to sell dope. I am working on this piece more attentively than the fifteen other things that I am supposed to be working on because I really do want to understand it. And as much difficulty as I am having with it, it is absolutely the kind of thing that I can only work out through writing. It has all of those complexities and ironies that I spoke about earlier.

As a writer, I am very interested in how stories come together and how things are told. I have learned from a lot of different people. Generally speaking in terms of black literature, I don't see a huge difference between the way black people tell stories and the way white people tell stories. There are exceptions, of course, but I can't imagine aside from race—and as Ralph Ellison says, "I know of no gene for culture"—how you can put John Wideman and Ernest Gaines in the same category of black literature without making an awful lot of concessions to style, and to philosophy. It doesn't make any sense. It is a convenient academic slump. Black literature as we know it has been powerful and important politically; unfortunately, it remains politically important. What we need to do is to fight the politics with politics, not with literature. And fight literature with *good* literature.

In good literature, I want a story that helps me to understand why people do what they do, what they believe, and how their beliefs influence their actions. I want something that makes sense. To me, a really good piece of literature will tell me what is behind the most stupid and irrational behavior—it may not make me see it as any less stupid or irrational, but it will make me understand that behavior, and it will slow down my judgment. Good literature may not change my judgment, but it will help me come to it more reluctantly. That is what I want in literature, and that is what I have tried to deliver in literature. Do I think I am a good writer? On my good days, ain't nobody better; on my bad days, better than most.

From

THE CHANEYSVILLE INCIDENT

We had dreamed away the day, he in delirium, I in reverie. From time to time he wakened to cough, from time to time I stirred to put more wood on the fire. The stove's mechanical clankings disappeared; what was left was a soft, eerie, almost undiscernible squeaky hissing hum, the sound of a drawn-out kiss. I drifted, recalling another time when I had sipped whiskey and listened to a fire's keening.

My eleventh birthday. A night in summer, the air warm enough, but tinged with the chill that always haunts the mountains. There was a strong wind aloft; the clouds were strung out like great hurrying ghosts.

We had been camped in the lee of a giant boulder, near a minor stream called Nigger Hollow Run, waiting for Uncle Josh White's dogs to catch the trail of some unfortunate raccoon. Uncle Josh himself sat stoically beyond the range of the firelight, pulling steadily at a bottle of Four Roses. Old Jack sat closer to the flames, sipping a toddy from a tin cup. I sat beside him, sipping from a tin cup of my own. Uncle Josh, as usual, was as silent as the tomb. Old Jack, as usual, was talking, but softly; he was telling a tale. I could not really hear him; I had had three or four toddies by that time, and all I could really do was to sit and hold the warm cup clutched against my belly, watching the flames dance against the backdrop of the night. His words came to me only in bits and snatches, but I had not needed to hear more; I knew the tale. He had told me the story twenty times by then, but he had only needed to tell me once, for at that first telling he had said that it was a tale that Moses

Washington had liked to tell, over and over again. And so I could sit by the campfire, hearing the words with only half my mind, filling in the details on my own, telling myself the story of a dozen slaves who had come north on the Underground Railroad, fleeing whatever horrors were behind them, and who had got lost just north of the Mason-Dixon Line, somewhere in the lower reaches of the County, and who, when they could no longer elude the men who trailed them with dogs and horses and ropes and chains, had begged to be killed rather than be taken back to bondage. But that night had been different; he had added something new. His voice had come clearly to me, coming, it had seemed, out of the flames: "Some say they give up. Some say they quit. White folks say it mostly, though I've heard some colored say it too. Bunch a sorry niggers, they say, too scared to fight, too scared to run, too scared to face slav'ry, too scared even to kill their own selves; couldn't even get away that way, lessen a white man done it for 'em. An' maybe that's the truth of it, though it seems to me you don't want to be judgin' folks too quick, or too hard. Maybe you can do it if you're white, but it strikes me a colored man oughta understand what it coulda been like, white folks all around you, an' no place to turn. But judgin' don't matter when you get to the bottom of it, on accounta don't nobody know what happened down there in the South County, or when, or even 'xactly where. I doubt the killin' part of it myself. On accounta they ain't dead. They're still here. Still runnin' from them dogs an' whatnot. I know, on accounta I heard 'em. I ain't never heard 'em that often—maybe five, six times in ma whole life. Funny times. I never heard 'em anytime when there wasn't snow on the ground, for instance. An' I ain't never heard 'em when I was listenin' for 'em special. Now I think on it, I only ever heard 'em when I was on the trail a somethin' else, an' I'd be listenin' for whatever I was after, jest settin' there lettin' the sound come to me, an' then I'd hear 'em. Wouldn't be no big noise. Wouldn't be nothin' like them sounds them dumb-butted white folks, don't know a ghost from a bed sheet, is all the time tellin' you ghosts make. On accounta they ain't ghosts; they ain't dead. They're jest runnin' along. An' the sound you hear is the sound of 'em pantin'. First time I heard 'em, I recall I was caught out in a storm, up along Barefoot Run. I thought I had time to make a kill an' get on back, but the wind shifted on me an' . . ."

Then he had called to me, his voice cracking, and I had risen from the chair and gone to him, had touched his forehead. The flesh had seemed hot enough to burn.

Later, I fed him stew, and then I filled his chipped enamel basin and had washed him as best I could, trying to be gentle with him despite the rough rag and lye soap I had to use, despite the embarrassed looks he gave me. Then I helped him use the old enamel chamber pot, hating what it did to him to be so helpless, hating the process, hating myself for hating it. I had escaped outside to empty the pot, and had found the ground covered with snow, the air clotted with flakes. And so I had turned and gone back inside, to tell him we had to go.

"No," he said. "No, Goddamnit. No."

"Jack . . ."

"I said no."

"You need a doctor," I said. "You need a hospital. That cough sounds like your guts are comin' out."

"I feel fine."

"You look like hell."

"I ain't never been pretty."

I turned away then and went to the stove. I started to put more wood in, but I realized that would be a step towards giving in. "Jack," I said. "You can't stay here."

"Hell I can't. I stayed here for fifty years. If I got sick, I took care a myself. I didn't need no hospital then, I don't need one now. Don't nobody do nothin' in the hospital 'cept die."

"It's startin' to snow," I told him. I let it go at that; he would know what it meant.

"You had to go out there to find that out? I could smell it." He started to cough again. I stepped across and stood above him while he coughed. He looked up at me over the rag he held clamped to his mouth, his eyes wide and guilty, as if he were a little boy who was being naughty. When he had finished I moved to clean the mucus from his face before he could even begin to do it for himself. And when it was over, when he lay back panting for breath, I took the rag away from him and went and threw it into the gathering darkness and the accumulating snow. Then I washed my hands. I did not look at him.

"Johnny," he said, "they'll kill me."

I spun around to face him. "God*damn*it, Jack, they don't kill people. They take care of 'em."

"White people, maybe."

"Jack, things have changed a little—"

"Listen to him: 'Things have changed.' I spent the best part a my life tryin' to teach you up from down an' left from sideways, an' now you come tryin' to tell me that things have changed to the point where they give a good Goddamn about what happens to a colored man." He was silent for a moment, and I thought he was getting ready to cough again, but he wasn't; he was thinking. "Johnny, sit down there." I hesitated. "Go on," he said. I shrugged, pulled out my chair, sat. "Do you recall when you got your hair cut the first time?"

"What does that—"

"Do you recall it? I don't mean when your mama first took the shears to you; I mean when you went to the barber the first time?"

"Sure," I said.

"What happened?"

"What do you mean, what happened? We went to the barber an' he cut my hair. You took me."

"Where'd we go?"

"Altoona. What—"

"An' after that first time, where'd you get your hair cut?"

"Everett. Jack, you know that as well as—"

"Well, now, as I recollect it, Altoona's pert near forty mile off, an' Evert's eight. An' this here is the county seat. You mean to tell me there wasn't no barbershops in the county seat?"

I didn't say anything.

"You know why you didn't go to none a them barbershops, Johnny? I'll tell you why. On accounta every colored man in this town knowed that if he was to walk in an' set down they'd tell him they didn't know how to cut a colored man's hair. Wasn't that they didn't *want* to, now; it was just that they didn't know how. An' a course it wasn't their fault that they didn't learn, on accounta after the third or fourth colored man come out 'thout gettin' his hair cut, didn't no more go in. Well, we coulda done a lotta things, if we'da been like some these folks nowadays, we'da probly burnt them barbershops to the gound. Maybe we shoulda. Folks now probly think we didn't even think about it, but we did. But then that didn't seem to make no sense. So what we done, Johnny, was we worked it out like it was some kinda ceremony down to the Legion—just like that, on accounta it was Bunk that thought it up, an' Bunk surely loves his Legion ceremonies. We kept it secret; wasn't moren ten, twelve of us knowed. What we done was to keep a real close watch on the young boys—wasn't never that many—an' soon as a colored boy looked like he was gettin' tall enough to go to his first real barber, we'd get together an' scratch up some way to carry him over the mountain to Altoona, so's he could get his hair cut by a colored man. After that, the white fella down to Evert was good enough; an' he sure as hell was smartern the barbers around here; a head a nappy hair didn't slow him down one bit. Now, we done that so you young boys wouldn't have to set there an' hear some damn peckerwood tell you that you was such a strange kinda animal that the same pair a scissors that cut a white man's hair wouldn't make a dent in yours. We didn't want you to have to hear that; figured you'd hear somethin' like it soon enough. Mose said we was all crazy. Said there wasn't no use puttin' it off. Said what we was doin' was lettin' boys go along thinkin' the world was one way when it wasn't, that this here town was one way when it was just about as near to the other as it could be. An' I think now maybe he was right; we shoulda let you find out. We shoulda let you bleed the same damn way we did every damn day; maybe then you wouldn't be tryin' to tell me I oughta go runnin' to the hospital jest to hear some white man tell me he don't know where a colored man's gizzard is at."

I shifted uncomfortably in the chair. I wanted to argue, but I couldn't. Because things that I had never really understood were suddenly coming clear: the time when Bill and I had decided that the river wasn't good enough for us and had scraped together the nickels and dimes with which to pay the admission to the Town's one swimming pool, and had set out to walk the three or four miles to get there, but had never made it because we had come across Uncle Bunk (who hadn't taken a day off in twenty years that anybody could recollect, but who for some reason had that day), who had asked us where we were going and, when we told him, had proceeded to tell us about the eye-burning chemicals in pool water, and to point out that we could swim in the river for free and buy sodas with the money. Or another time: when, after a football game, I had been heading for one of the high school hangouts, a coffee shop on Juliana Street, and Old Jack had appeared as if by magic, and had asked me to help him with some odd or end, and had kept me with him by spinning out one of his long, involved tales—which had more attraction for me than any milk shake—and by the time we were finished, the time for milk shakes was past. Eventually, of course, we had come to know that we were not welcome at the swimming pool or in that particular coffee shop, but by then we had been scarred by so many of the little assumptions and presumptions that go with dormant racism or well-meaning liberalism that a little overt segregation was almost a relief.

CECIL BROWN

CECIL BROWN was born in North Carolina and educated at Columbia University and the University of Chicago. He is the author of three books, which include his critically acclaimed novel *The Life and Loves of Mr. Jiveass Nigger* (1969) and a memoir, *Coming Up Down Home* (1993). He recently received his Ph.D. in English and is currently teaching at the University of California at Berkeley.

THINK WRITING IS A GOOD WAY to ease into living and to understand the inevitability of death. I love oral culture, but oral culture does not assure that somebody will remember your words. If you write a book, there will always be some remembrance. I think it would be horrible to live your life and think that nothing will live after you are gone.

We lived on my grandfather's farm in the South when I was coming up. I had to travel real far to get to school, so far that the kids called me Swamp Rabbit. I told my mom about it, and she told me that rabbits were very smart, so I wrote a story. One time my brother and I tried to get lost so that we could find our way home according to the *Boy Scout Guide*; we went into the woods, we made a compass, and we made a light by taking something shiny like aluminum foil and putting it in a can with a candle inside. We were trying to see how long we could survive in the woods. A little ways into our journey we saw a bear. Well, I'll tell you, we found our way back home quick, and figured that we had survived about long enough! When I got home I wrote a story about that experience. I brought the story to school and the kids liked it. I realized that writing was a way to get attention, which I really wanted because kids were calling me the Swamp Rabbit, you know. The story wasn't any kind of masterpiece or anything, but it was my own experience.

When I was coming up I didn't know anything else was happening in the world other than the southern black experience. Being young in the South meant having complete freedom. One time my mother was talking with a white friend of hers in town. I asked the white woman if she was a "cracker." I said, "Miss Shepard, are you a cracker? Mama said you were a cracker!" I didn't understand that crackers were another race of people. It was just a word I had heard used to describe certain people. Of course, both my mother and Miss Shepard were embarrassed, but the point is that we as children were free to ask questions, to play with white children, and to do other sorts of things without necessarily being restricted by race. As we got older we started getting slapped for certain things. When I was about twelve or thirteen I was playing tag with a bunch of other children. This white girl was chasing me, and when she caught up with me, she kissed me on my hand. Just then, my mother came to pick up me and my brother. I knew she had seen the white girl kiss me, but she didn't say anything about it right away. When we got in the car, my mother slapped me and told me not to ever do *that* again. I didn't understand at first, but slowly I began to catch on.

I started paying closer attention to the stories being told by older people about "the black and white thing." I knew then that I would no longer be able to say and do certain things. There were many older black people in my life who were very intelligent and who commanded a strong presence. Even though some of them were illiterate, they were still beautiful, mysterious, and somehow very dangerous. When I began to see these same people saying "Yes, Ma'am" and "Yessir" to little children, I knew something was wrong. I felt betrayed.

My grandfather worked very hard for his farmland. There were a lot of deer on that land, and when we moved there, my daddy let this white man hunt on our land for free. I had the idea that we should charge this white man, but my daddy wasn't going for it. He thought he was building a nice, friendly relationship with a white man. I knew there was no way that same white man would have let us hunt on his land. So by the time I moved up north at sixteen years old, I was angry and I felt slighted about what was clearly an unfair racial dynamic.

Originally I had wanted to be a saxophone player. I had a horn, but I lost it somewhere the summer after I moved to New York. That's when I started thinking about being a writer. When I first went back south after moving north, I told my friend that being a writer was what the future held. I told him that from the likes of what I saw in New York, we should forget about being musicians because being writers was going to be much more happening. I saw black people in the Village reading poetry and talking about things that they liked, things they didn't like, and things that they hated. I thought that there was a tremendous amount of power in being able to say what you felt through writing. It was all that much more powerful to have people actually listen to what you were saying and for them to feel something too.

The first thing I published in New York was a letter to this journalist who had written something about black people that had made me angry. I sent my letter to the publication he wrote for and they called me back to tell me that the issue was too big for a letter and that they wanted to make it into an article. I wasn't thinking about writing so much as I was thinking about *responding*. I had been compelled to write a response to that journalist based on my emotional reaction to what he had written. He had misunderstood southerners in his piece, and I felt incredibly protective of the southern experience. I thought that any white person in the North who knew black people should like us. There were so many white people in the South who didn't like black people. I didn't think that northern whites had the right, or the privilege rather, to dislike the southern black. I considered us (southern blacks) to be on the forefront of the battle. I couldn't imagine anybody not being conscious of that, especially northern whites because they had such a reputation for progress and liberal views.

There is a certain level of creativity involved with responding to something you feel angry about. I think it is really unfortunate when people can't understand the meaning and value of protest literature. When we look back on the history of African-American folk and literary culture, we see that some of the most poignant and beautiful writing came out of the protest periods. Writers like Richard Wright, James Baldwin, and Ralph Ellison were really responding to and arguing against an unequal racial situation. It is difficult to outline the criteria for protest literature, but one of the most important criteria is the ability to create a voice that brings forth a strong sense of pride as well as a strong sense of character. You cannot write protest literature in an honest and compelling way unless you have character. Because in order to protest in a way that is believable, you have to be able to stand behind your words; you have to stand behind the sum of your words, which is "I'm better than that foolish line of racism. I'm not going to fall underneath it."

Over the years, black culture has in some ways lost our raison d'être. We are losing our center and have come frighteningly close to falling underneath racism. That is why I have a lot of faith in rappers today because I feel that rappers represent the same sort of anger that I was feeling during the sixties when I first started writing. I love folklore and the beautiful and imaginitive way that words roam through literature, but I also feel that black literature tries to rise above the oppression in an unhealthy way. Rappers are combining the spoken word with the undying truth and emotion of music, while adding anger to fuel the fire.

When *The Life and Loves of Mr Jiveass Nigger* came out, I was at the forefront of the breaking ground for black literature. I sometimes wish that I had been a rapper then because I had an explosive energy that was very arrogant and righteous, and at the time, I felt like orally declaring more often than I felt like writing. After the book came out I wouldn't even give interviews. I used to tell reporters and journalists to kiss my ass all the time. I didn't care what or how people thought of me, I was doing my own thing and it felt good. I had a sort of iconoclastic way of looking at things; white people were not giving me a language with which I could express my pain, so I was going to create my own language. It took me a long time before I realized that I'd better straighten up and fly right if I wanted to be taken seriously as a writer or as a person. I realized that I had to let go of some of my rebellion. Some, but not all. Human nature reserves the instinct to strike out against people who are being disrespectful. So although I understood that I would have to curtail some of my rebellious attitude, I still maintained a righteous reserve.

I have always enjoyed reading things that I have written. It may sound narcissistic, but if I explain something clearly through writing it is always helpful to read it again and again. When I write something well it feels as though I am stopping time in a way so I can give myself the chance to really do it right. A whole lot of things happen in the course of a day, and when I sit down to write, I organize things around each other. I recollect dangers that I have passed when I write, and other various experiences and ideas that I am able to put into perspective in the quietude of my writing space. There is an incredible pull to go back into my past when I begin to write, it's almost like a drug. I have a fear, though, that if I write about something in a certain way and use a particular combination of words, then I will never be able to imagine it, think about it, or talk about it in any other way. Writing really makes things concrete, and being a writer requires a lot of courage.

I come from an oral family; southerners are *all* oral—they talk about you and magnify who you are. If you live in a southern African-American family, you live in about four thousand different versions of who you are. There are things that happened in my life that I couldn't possibly remember, but enough relatives tell stories about those things to make me feel as though I do remember! And one story will get told over many many times in an array of amazing different viewpoints. You know, the actual event happens once, but folks be telling the stories four hundred times! The essence and the tellability of the story is so beautiful. And because it is generally older people talking about younger people, the story calls for honorability and credence. If you have the good fortune to be a story's subject, it doesn't actually matter whether or not you remember anything from the actual experience, because it is far more important to listen to the perceptions of those around you than it is to listen to your own perceptions—there's no truth in the way you *remember* doing it, the truth is in how they remember *you doing it!* Stories tell you how close you are to somebody, how much they love you, and how much they enter into your world and you enter into theirs.

When I came up north I can remember shedding my oral tradition, and I knew that I could never get it back. After I had been living in the North for a while, one of my teachers invited me to play chess with him. I brought all of my friends with me because in the South everyone does everything together. Individuality is a phenomen to southerners because the South is very community oriented—as long as you could call somebody's name, he or she was part of you. The longer I lived in the North, the more of an individual I became. I wasn't sure then and I still don't know whether that is good or not. Because I think about how when the slaves were brought over to this country, they all came in one group, and they recognized that fact and must have shared a huge commonality of feelings. I imagine that feeling would last a long time and is perhaps the basis of southern community.

In addition to the general influences of the North, writing also taught me about individuality; it taught me how to respond to the individual call. Writing was something that I couldn't do with my buddies, or with anyone else. It was difficult to leave my sense of community, but I also felt that I could give it a voice. As African-American literature progresses, it becomes harder to speak for a group or to speak for anyone, and it is not perceived as an act of kindness. Richard Wright thought he was speaking for masses of black people, and it was a generous act. No writer is really able to do that anymore without being politically attacked in some way.

After my first novel came out I began to feel like an individual: I tried to be as different as I possibly could from other black people. There were many things that I didn't like about black people at that time and I wanted to stand out from the rest. But the more I tried, the more I became the epitome of what, not who, white people *thought* black people were, which served as a very interesting dichotomy. Black people have tended to agree with whatever has been said about us that makes some headway in the world and that passes with the white man—it could be literature, sports, whatever—but we often gauge our success by and defer our individuality to the chosen black representatives. I thought that by being a writer I was being an individual, but my first novel's success and the attention it granted caused me to fall into the throes of white people's measure of success.

It used to be that no matter how great you were as a black person, unless you could write a book, then you weren't anything. Because the writing implied that you were able to rise out of illiteracy and meet the white man. If the book became accepted, then the writer became a representative for all black people, like Frederick Douglass and Booker T. Washington. It was, and to some degree still is, about meeting the standards of white society. We need to learn self-acceptance before we can move ahead. At the same time, there are aspects and behaviors within our culture that we appreciate and that white people don't even think about. Black women raise children on their own, stand by their men, and still become successful in diverse fields—as a culture, we recognize and appreciate that. Or a preacher who delivers a knockout sermon every Sunday—we care about that. We need that.

As a writer, I think about a deep and responsive audience. Sometimes I feel that I am creating an audience; trying to bring people in to where I am with the hope that they will show some empathy for whatever situation or feeling I am writing about. Other times I am not worried about bringing people in—and I like being where I am with only myself to please.

I promised myself this year that I wouldn't talk about anything that I haven't yet written, because sometimes talking expends the energy I need to write. Before I talked about something, I wanted to have written about it so that it would be past tense in conversation. I broke that promise immediately. The interaction with other voices is too important.

From

THE LIFE AND LOVES OF MR. JIVEASS NIGGER

The Spirit of the Father

I swear 'fo God this is the cussinges' man ever born, he must've been cussing when he came into this world, when his mother, Miss Lillybelle Washington, gave birth to this heathen the first thing he said must've been a cuss word, he probably cussed out the midwife and his mother and anybody else who happened to be in sight, cussed them out for bringin' him into the world, he is that kind of man, you know. . . . There ain't a soul in this community he ain't cussed out, hardly a dog or cat either. But the Lord is gonna visit this nigger, you watch and see, he's gonna visit this nigger. When I met him, when I first laid eyes on this nigger he was cussing, out in the street cussing with my brothers, and I said to myself, why is that nigger always using cuss words? So I thought it was just youth, just being young, and I was foolish enough to up and marry that fool. He tole me after we got married he was gonna stop cussing, and you know the stranges' thing is that he did. And three months later, he cuss old man Lennon into a blue streak. Old man Lennon ain't never bother no body, that old man been walking around this town for forty years picking up junk in his wheelbarrow and taking it home to see what use he could fine out of it, and he happened to come by the house and this nigger of mine claimed the man picked up his hammer. Lord God Almighty, did he cuss that poor man out. I can't stand no cussing man, I don't like no cussing man, Lord gib me any kind of man, a short, square-headed man, a ugly man, any kind of man, but don't give me no cussing man. I got experience to prove this: that there ain't but one thing a cussing man is good for and that is cussing. There is one thing about a cussing man that you can bet your bottom dollar on and that is he will cuss, and if he don't cuss, grits ain't grocery, eggs ain't poultry, and Mona Lisa was a man. But the Lord gonna visit that nigger, the Lord, or somebody, gonna visit him, because you can't go through life cussing out everybody, everything you see, you just can't do that, and get away with it. Or am I a fool? That nigger cussed out God himself, yes he did. I was telling him he should go to church, you know once in a while, not all the time, just once in a while, and that nigger broke bad and said that the Lord could kiss his black ass. But the Lord ain't gonna kiss no nigger's black ass, or if he do kiss it then that nigger knows something I don't know and wanna find out about pretty quick. My grandmother, Dennier Saint Marie, she's dead and gone now, she tole me when I was nothing but a five-year-old. Tole me to never marry a cussing man. One of her boyfriends, she had aplenty, she had three children by black men and three by white men, and some by an Indian too (we got all kinds of blood in us), one of her boyfriends, who use to wear that straw hat that put you in the mind of a tap dancer, he had just come into the gate and we was all sitting on the porch, it was a Sunday afternoon, and there was some white and red roses in the garden and we had picked some red roses and pinned them to our clothes in honor of the fact that our mother was alive, it was Easter Sunday you know and Gramma had a white one for her blouse, and this boyfriend of hers came bursting into the gate, just cussing like a nigger, I mean he was *talking*, but every few words was a cuss word, and Gramma just turned politely to him and said would you excuse yourself, there's some ladies present, and he said you never heard shit before, everybody shits, and Gramma said you better get your filthy ass out of this garden. And when he left, she turned to me (it seems like she was speaking only to me even though there were about twelve people present) and said, honey don't ever marry a cussing man, because a cussing man ain't good for nothing but one thing—and that's cussing. Now those was some words I should have heeded, but I didn't heed them, I went right out and the first man I looked at good I married (because I loved him) and he turned out to be a cussing man. I don't care what my sons be, I don't care really what they do, just so they don't grow up cussing everything they lay eyes on. I can't stand no cussing man. When I hear a man cussing, my insides go to pieces. That's one thing about white men. They shor don't cuss like niggers. Of course, a poor white peck will cuss. A poor white peck will cuss worse'n a nigger. I am talking about white men who ain't poor like them pecks. I guess a nigger man cuss because he is so poor and ain't nothin' but a nigger. But a nigger should learn not to cuss, he should learn not to cuss too much. To tell you the truth, there ain't nothin' wrong with cussing. I do a little bit myself, but there is somethin' wrong with a nigger cussing *all the time.* There is somethin' wrong with that kind of nigger, somethin' done gone wrong deep down inside of that nigger, if everything he says is a blasphemous cuss word, if every time he opens his mouth it's a cocksucker, motherfucker-down-the-ditch-up-the-ditch-longheaded-sonofabitch, or if he is always saying, I wish I was dead, I'm gonna be glad when I die (like some niggers I know), and things like this, then there is something deep down wrong with that nigger and he oughta go to church and testify. But this man won't testify, he above testifying, he rather cuss, I guess cussing is his way of testifying. I can understand that, I just hope God understands it.

■

A Brief History

Let us backtrack a moment. The most salient characteristic of George Washington's early childhood (and, indeed, his early youth) was his *individuality*. This talent of his, the almost fanatical ability to remain *different* against all odds, was apparent even at birth: young George Washington was born on the Fourth of July in the year of Our Lord nineteen hundred and forty-four in his father's bed, which had been recently vacated by George's grandfather, who had to flee the county for having (allegedly) whipped a fellow—Josh Smith, to be exact—with a slab because the said Josh had accused George's grandfather of having fathered a child by Josh's poor wife. George was assisted in entering this world by his grandmother, a squatty little woman with very definite strains of Indian blood, who will swear to this day that when George Washington came out of the womb he was grinning. No one knew what he was grinning about. Except, of course, George himself. His grandmother claimed he was the blackest baby she'd ever seen come into the world, and later on, when George was older, she went on to offer the opinion that he was the *blackest child she'd ever seen period*. There is some truth in this, for the child was extremely dark, and it was this unusual hue that led many members of the family to think that he was destined to become, as it were, the black sheep of the family. But the most amazing change occurred to George when he was in the last of his fifth year: his skin began to get lighter, until, at age twelve, he possessed the finest shade of brown complexion imaginable, and it was this complexion that he kept for the balance of his days. No one really understood why the change took place at the time that it did, or really what it signified. It is, however, a small matter, and besides it is only his mother and grandmother who still insist that George Washington was once *really* black. His mother, furthermore, is very pleased with the brown hue of her first-born.

When George was only two, his father, Jake, who, incidentally, was the one who earmarked him with the name George, went off to prison, in very much the same fashion as some young fathers were at that time going off to war—that is to say, reluctantly. With the exception of brief visits, George did not see his father for a great number of years, but he was not without a father figure. Quite to the contrary, young Washington lived in a household that was abounding with male models: his four uncles, ranging from age seventeen to twenty-eight, who shared the house with the rest of the family (twelve or thirteen or fourteen, depending on whether you counted Buckcaesar or Siren as dogs or humans), were very excellent models, indeed. Illiterate, generous, intuitive, simple, and hopelessly backwards, they were probably some of the finest men in the whole world. From them little Washington learned at an exceptionally early age how to swear, talk about women, talk *to* women, how to farm, hunt, fish, avoid unnecessary work, how to relax, how to tell when a white cracker is trying his best to get something for nothing (which is most of the time), and how to look at a nappy head woman and tell if the sap's running. Like all true students, George outgrew his teachers and became something his uncles never dreamed of: he became literate, which is to say, he became a voracious reader of any piece of printed matter he could lay hands on. Because he was such a lover of reading, and being the only one in the household who could read (with the exception of his mother), it was his task and pleasure to read any bit of mail, be it a letter from Aunt Mabel in Philly or third-class advertisement sheets, aloud for all to hear, in very much the fashion of the town crier. He was much appreciated by the family for his learning and gentlemanly bearing, and was much loved by all. And thus he spent his early years until the age of twelve, at which point he was (un)fortunately seduced by a wayward and voluptuous aunt. After this initial loss of innocence, the boy took to laying out with women, and to heavy usage of rot-gut liquor, cigarettes, and reefers. When he was only eight, his teacher once asked the class who the father of our country was, and of course George was quick to shout out his name—proudly. In a brief five years, however, all this optimism was shot to hell, for George's most favorite expression of his philosophical view of life was summed up in a conscious parody of Ecclesiastes' famous dictum: "I have seen all the works that are done under the sun; and, behold, all *is* jive and vexation of the spirit." Many a night he lay his gun down on an oak, and stared up at the stars and, wondering what it all meant, lost his consciousness in a spiritual transcendence that would leave him shivering and scratching about, two hours later, for his soul. Upon recovering, he would chant, "Jive, it's all jive."

WESLEY BROWN

W

ESLEY BROWN is the author of two novels, *Tragic Magic* (1978) and *Darktown Strutters* (1994), and two plays, *Boogie Woogie and Booker T.* (1987) and *Life During Wartime* (which received five AUDELCO awards for excellence in black theater in 1992), and has coedited two multicultural anthologies, *Imagining America* (1991) and *Visions of America* (1992). Brown has taught at Hunter College, Sarah Lawrence College, Columbia University, and Princeton University and is currently an associate professor of English at Rutgers University.

WRITING WAS FIRST about getting what I needed to say out into the world. A few years later I realized that I also wanted for it to be heard.

Writing for me comes out of my experience in Mississippi during the summer of 1965. It was a defying moment to be involved in a movement that was so connected with the lives of black people in rural Mississippi. Although I am from New York, my parents are both originally from the South. The year before I went to Mississippi, two civil rights workers who were involved with the Student Nonviolent Coordinating Committee came to the school that I was attending. Up until then all that I had seen surrounding the civil rights movement in the South had been on television, so seeing these two civil rights workers who had actually put their bodies so directly in harm's way for the movement was incredibly powerful and compelling.

I had always been very politically conscious of what was going on during the sixties, not only in the South but in New York, where there was also a lot of political ferment as well. Nineteen sixty-four was the year of the Freedom Summer in Mississippi and the riots in Harlem. As all of these events were going on, there was a lot of turmoil inside of me to respond and to lend myself to the Cause. Individuals like Martin Luther King, Jr., Bob Moses, and Fannie Lou Hamer had obviously been very inspiring, but it wasn't until I was in college that I was able to make the decision to really act.

When I decided to go south, I didn't yet know what I was going to do with my life; all I knew was that I felt the need to be connected to the movement in some way. It wasn't that I was disassociated with the fight for black people's rights, because I was connected to it by virtue of being black; it was more about being at the core of what was going on and being able to *touch* it. The atmosphere in the South at that time was far more dramatic than what was going on in New York; the South was the *pulse* of the movement—the center of gravity.

The two SNCC workers had participated in the 1964 Freedom Summer and had come to my college to recruit black students to join in the next summer's voter registration drive. They became the cord that connected me to what I had been feeling so strongly about. I went to Mississippi that following summer, in 1965, and stayed there for four months. The experience changed my life in every conceivable way. The person who I am, and who I continue to become, has predominately been shaped by that very brief period of time in my life. The seeds of wanting to write began in Mississippi.

I had always been a very private and interior person by temperament, so I think that my sensibility had already lent itself to someone who might write. I've always been very comfortable living alone, living within myself, and spending time in my own head—writing seemed to be a natural outgrowth for me, but it wasn't until my experience working with SNCC and the Mississippi Freedom Democratic Party that I began to feel that there was something I needed to express, and that writing was the way I would do it.

Deciding to write had everything to do with seeing the way black people and the events of the movement were being portrayed in the media, and how those images were completely at odds with the way that I saw and felt about those very same people and experiences. I chose to write to find out what I believed, but also because I realized that my perception of how the world felt to me was important, and that no one would be able to tell my story in the same way that I told it. I knew intuitively that writing would provide me with the opportunity to have my say without it being mediated by a second party.

During SNCC meetings and discussions about what courses of action might be taken in terms of demonstrations and organizing, I found that some of the more articulate speakers had the effect of silencing people. There was a general feeling in SNCC that the more articulate speakers from northern and elite universities had unwittingly created a very clear class division within the group. There were leaders like Bob Moses, who would have the effect of both intimidating people and making them want to speak out for the first time. This played an important role in making people realize that silence is a form of complicity in keeping things the way they are. In order to gain the attention of someone, or to make someone aware, there has to be a spoken demand—otherwise the assumption of consent will be made. All of us who were in SNCC grappled with issues of class and race, as well as relationships between men and women. The key to understanding these issues was in identifying our voices. I later discovered that writing was a way to keep my spoken voice alive.

As a writer I have always been fascinated by the type of writing that uses rich imagery, metaphor, and improvisation as a way to invoke the speech of black people. There has always been a desire and a craving among black people for the Word, whether it is written or spoken, and I know that I carry that desire within me. During slavery it was unlawful to teach a black person to read; it was considered a subversive act. Frederick Douglass believed that learning to read was an important aspect of freedom, and that by extension, he had the ability to create himself through the act of speech, and of writing his story. If there are black people who cannot be brought into a dialogue with a writer through the specific act of writing, there is still the act of speaking, and writing is simply another way of speaking. There will always be a certain level of tension between writing and speaking among black people because of our precarious relationship to English, for the English language as we now know it was once an unknown language that was rammed down our throats, which we then had to figure out how to bend and take apart so we would be able to use it.

After my experience in Mississippi, I went back to college in New York, and after graduating in 1968, I tried to find a way to get back involved with SNCC. At that time, however, SNCC was in complete disarray, and it didn't look as though I would be able to reconnect. Alternately, I became involved with the Black Panther party. New York City had become crazy and was not the place to be, so I moved to Rochester and helped form a chapter of the Black Panther party there. For the next year or two I was actively involved with the party and worked on various educational programs for black children. The stress and strain of the chapter's protests and actions were both physically and emotionally draining, and we burnt ourselves out rather quickly. The chapter members then retreated from all of the confusion to pick up our lives again. It was at that point that I remember reading two books that particularly influenced my writing life—*The Man Who Cried I Am* by John A. Williams and *Yellow Back Radio Broke-Down* by Ishmael Reed.

John A. Williams's book was about the struggles of a black American male writer who journeys to Europe in search of his identity. I was profoundly moved by that book because its central theme was that the writing itself was the key to the writer's identity. Ishmael Reed's book offered an intelligent satirical bend on America, and his ability to pillory everything in sight was incredibly refreshing at a time when there were a lot of proscriptions being offered about how black people were supposed to behave; what was *black* behavior and what wasn't. Reed's voice sent up all of that orthodoxy and used the stiff proscribed attitudes as a source of humor. I thought to myself: If this guy can do this, then that allows all sorts of possibilities for me as a writer without my having to feel that I'm under the supervision of some committee telling me what I can and can't write. Reed's work was very important in freeing me up to feel that I could write about anything as long as I was being honest with myself.

In 1965, when I was in Mississippi, I was called for a physical by my draft board in New York. I had it changed to Memphis, but I never showed up for the physical and was declared delinquent. Later that year, I applied for conscientious objector status on political and philosophical grounds, but the Supreme Court had decided that they would grant CO status only to men who had religious training in an institutional setting that was responsible for the conscientious objection. The CO status could not be a personal code unless there was a religious institutional affiliation. When the draft board found out that I had been arrested for demonstrating in Mississippi and had spent seven days in jail, they changed my classification from delinquent to 1Y, which meant that I had a criminal case pending. My classification remained 1Y until 1966, when Lyndon Johnson stipulated that anyone who was in college—in good standing—would be granted a deferment until they graduated, which for me was in 1968. That same year, I was drafted but refused to report for induction. And on January 27, 1972, I was sentenced to three years at the federal penitentiary in Lewisburg, Pennsylvania, where I spent the next year and a half.

Before I was sentenced, I had started to write a coming-of-age novel that I continued working on while I was in prison. When I got out, a friend of mine encouraged me to write about my experience in Lewisburg. I really had not been interested in dealing with that experience until I realized that it was a crucial part of the story that I had already been working on. Much like my own experience, the main character in *Tragic Magic* had just served two years in prison and then is reunited with an old friend of his. However, the story was fictionalized a great deal. Generally, first novels are often more autobiographical than later works because as a writer, you are still trying to figure out how to do what it is that you are doing. In writing about a personal experience, there is a feeling of safety in not venturing too far from what you truly know.

I chose to write *Tragic Magic* as a novel because I felt that writing the story as straight autobiography did not seem to offer as many possibilities as fiction could. I wanted to write in a way that utilized my strong suits—my imagination, and my own way of playing with language. It was more appealing to me to move outside of my own life and to create a world than to be bound by just what I had experienced. I think that what is considered the truth, even in an autobiographical sense, is selective and distorted. In that vein, I felt that it would be a more interesting way of telling the truth if I took advantage of the latitude offered by my imagination and not limit myself to the specific details of my life.

The period between finishing *Tragic Magic*—when I had to let the characters go—and when the novel was published was about a year. By then, I was not connected to the book in the same way that I had been while I was writing it, so the feeling of gratification at the novel's positive public reception was not as immediate. The relationship between myself and what I am writing is special but not better than the relationship between myself and the people who read what I write. It's just different. The intense relationship between myself and what I am writing ends once I'm finished, but the relationship between myself and readers is continuous. I have barely glanced at *Tragic Magic* in years. In a way, it feels like it was written by someone else because I am at such a different place in my life than I was when I first started writing it. Yet I have an ongoing dialogue with many people who have read and have been affected by the book.

I have never seen writing as a profession: I felt that it was something that I needed to do whether or not anybody other than myself ever read what I wrote. I didn't even think about compensation when I first started writing, and the way that *Tragic Magic* was published was a combination of luck and timing. In 1973, while I was still working on the novel, a friend of mine told me about an M.A. program in writing at City University of New York, which didn't make any sense to me at all, since I was already writing. He suggested that the program might provide a good way to get a teaching job in the future. On a lark, I sent a chapter of the novel, which was read by Donald Barthelme, who was teaching there at the time, and I was accepted into the program.

Later on, Susan Sontag, who was also teaching at CUNY, sent some chapters of my book to an editor, Ted Solotaroff, at Bantam Books. He was interested and asked if I could send him more. By that time, the novel was just about complete, so I sent him the rest, and shortly thereafter he offered me a contract. Since Bantam was a paperback publishing house, they wanted to sell it to a hardcover house first and then bring it out in paperback later. At that time, Toni Morrison was a senior editor at Random House. She bought the book, and *Tragic Magic* came out in hardcover from Random House in 1978. Working with Toni Morrison was a wonderful experience. I had read all of her work up until that point— *The Bluest Eye*, *Sula*—and *Song of Solomon* had just come out. I was a huge admirer of her work, so it was an honor to have her take such an interest in *Tragic Magic*. I remember her telling me that I had a very distinct voice, which was quite a compliment coming from her.

Within the next five years I drafted a second novel, which Toni Morrison tried to get a contract for at Random House, but she was not able to get enough support. After it was turned down by various other publishing houses, I ended up setting it aside for a while. Some years later, after I had been teaching at Rutgers University for eleven years, a friend of mine, Steven Schrader, who is also the publisher of Cane Hill Press, asked me if I had anything in manuscript form that he could take a look at. I showed him this manuscript that, in an entirely different form, ultimately became *Darktown Strutters*. I've taken a long time to write the two novels that have been published because writing takes a long time, and cannot be rushed. Especially if you have other things to do—like make a living.

Literature is equipment for living. It helps me to make sense of where I am in the world. It shows me how the world feels, not just what it looks like. Writing has helped me to discover and define myself, and probably represents my best efforts to become the human being I like to think I am.

From
TRAGIC MAGIC

I told my folks I was going to see Otis at his job and then go to a disco. Debra gave me a ride to the station and I caught the subway into Manhattan. The train pulled in as I bought my token, and I was able to get inside just as the doors closed. The feeling that I was being locked up again gripped me. I was very uneasy and my face must have betrayed that because I noticed a few people staring at me. When I looked back at them, their eyes darted away like peas not wanting to get involved in a shell game. By the time the train reached my stop, the sound of the wheels against the rails had my ears pretty well dummied up. The train made a jerking stop, almost throwing me to the floor. But not forgetting my inmate training, I didn't get uptight. Like the hacks in the joint, the Metropolitan Transit Authority was harassing me, trying to get me to react. But I remained cool and got through the doors just before they closed.

I wondered how it was going to be seeing Otis again. Would he be overly self-conscious about his hand and resent my dropping in on him without warning? In a way I hoped this would be his attitude. He had been such a smooth specimen of manhood that I had to see if the loss of a hand had diminished any of his luster.

At Eighth Avenue a man snapped at me like a cat-o'-nine-tails hungry for the taste of flesh.

"*Muhammad Speaks*, brotherman!"

"No, thanks, I speak for myself."

"You're wrong, my brother. You can't speak for yourself until you have submitted to the truth."

"I didn't say I wouldn't submit to the truth. Only the newspaper."

"My brother, *Muhammad Speaks* is the truth!"

"I see."

"No, I don't think you do see, my brother. If you did, you would buy a copy of the paper."

"I'll get one from you some other time."

"Why wait, good brother? The hour is drawing late for the black man."

"I've always been late anyway."

"For a quarter you can find out what it's like to be on time."

"No, that's all right."

"That's the story of the black man in America. Always running from the truth."

"You sure about that?"

"Is pig pork?"

"That's the rumor."

"Brotherman, how long have you been asleep?"

"Oh, ever since you started trying to sell me that newspaper."

"You better wake up, brother. I have a message for you if you'd just open up your dead ears and submit. But you talking like a Negro now. And when you a NeeGrow that means you need to grow!"

"There's probably still some hope for me, then."

He shook his head, dropped away from me, and moved on to someone else.

Farther down the block some sounds scissored into me. Suddenly I found myself in the thick of a knotted ring of kids in front of a record store. They were winding to the sounds like a set of drunken propellers and mimicking the words of the records coming from the outside speakers. And they were together, too, pumping up swift on the balls of their feet, then jabbing their knees out and peddling themselves into a flirtation walk. Every slip in a shoulder, backbone, or hip came off with a stroke of finesse.

Watching them made me wonder about the origin of such dances as the Bop, Philly Dog, Boogaloo, Boston Monkey, Shing-a-ling, Skate, Fat Man, Push and Pull, Funky Chicken, and Penguin. Where did they come from? And how did they spread once they arrived? Maybe a dance is like an idea whose time has come. If it is, maybe it comes into town unawares in the brown bag of a churchgoing woman. And after stealing out of there it shops around for the right body to put the wobble on. And then, before something that was nobody's business becomes everybody's business, the new dance is good news in some unsuspecting soul's muscles and joints.

It struck me that a possible strategy for the race lay in the unpredictable way dances whistle-stop from city to city. If those who had an idea wouldn't tell until it was tapped into their backbones, then it would make more sense to everybody because the idea, like a dance, would be a permanent fixture in their lives. And once someone learned the steps of a new thought, he or she would be a courier for an idea whose time had come.

In keeping with my analysis, watching those kids dance began to trigger movement in me. Having been a child prodigy of Balling the Jack, the Eagle Rock, and the Camel Walk, I was getting the urge to twist out of the everyday run-of-the-mill and flirt with untried orbits.

"Hey, my man," I said, stepping forward, "can I get in on this?"

"Sure, come on and get yourself a step."

So, for a moment, I was a mean rudder knifing through the elements and wasn't to be held in check. But as a quarter-of-a-century-old relic, I didn't want to blow the hoochie-coochie feeling those kids had cornered. So I made my exit.

Four large illuminated letters spelling WHIP hung vertically alongside the building. From the looks of it, they also seemed to spell out what was responsible for the shape it was in. On the third floor of the walk-up a woman sat at a switchboard behind a glass enclosure.

"May I help you?" she asked.

"I'm here to see Otis Edwards."

"Is he expecting you?"

"No, but I'm a friend of his."

"What's your name?"

"Melvin Ellington."

"He's still in the studio. Why don't you have a seat while I call in and tell him you're here."

"Thank you." A security guard was slouched in a chair reading a newspaper. He gave me the benefit of a brief surveillance and went back to his reading.

"Ain't this a blip!" It was Otis. A shaved head dotted with pores and blending into a ripe plum face stuck out of a red turtleneck shirt. The end of the right sleeve was buttoned neatly across, concealing his nub. He had gotten thicker through the chest and shoulders, but was still tapered off lean from the waist on down.

I got up to greet him, extending my right hand. Realizing he couldn't shake my hand, I clumsily gripped his arm with both hands and smiled weakly.

"How you been, Otis?"

"Ain't no need a kickin, Mouth," he said, obviously enjoying my feeble attempt to appear as though I noticed nothing different about him. "You knew that I lost my hand in the Nam, didn't you?"

"Yeah, it's just that seeing it for the first time is sort of . . ."

"Well, don't worry about it. You'll get used to it. I have." He probably dug the hell out of acting this scene out with anyone who tried to be natural around him and ended up coming off exactly the opposite. It was small compensation for what he'd lost, but he probably took payback in whatever form it came. "How'd you know where to find me?" he asked.

"I ran into Pauline and Alice at Rocky's and they told me . . . I hope you don't mind me coming."

"No, I don't mind. I'm glad you came. It's been a long time. Almost six years, ain't it?"

"Yeah, just about."

"What's this I hear about you going to jail for not going in the service?"

"You heard right."

"When you get out?"

"Today."

"Shit! We got to hang out then. It's almost time for me to get off, so lay here a minute while I take care of a few things."

When we got out into the street, there was a group of people at the corner bunched like a skyline near an ashcan. Flames spiraled out of the can before breaking off into smoke. A few feet away a short, chunky man holding a guitar was sitting on a milk crate against the side of a building. He began to play, and his fingers moved over the strings with the delicacy of a daddy-longlegs spider.

"Hey, let's check this out," Otis said. "This cat is always out here playing. He's bad!" Then the man began to sing.

> "I'm a man
> M, man

A, a child
N, non-spoiled
I'm a man."

The authority with which he sang those lyrics made my skin shiver. When he finished, someone from the huddled group of people took a bag from underneath his coat, pulled out a greasy piece of chicken, and passed the bag around. Barbecue sauce slipped from lips and dripped down chins.

"Excuse my hands," someone said, passing a greasy chicken wing.

"Your hands don't make me no nevermind as long as I get me a piece of this gospel bird."

"Hey, who's got the part that goes over the fence?" The way they ate that chicken told me that they not only shared food but the same abuses and jokes.

"Let's split," Otis said.

"Wait a minute. I want to ask him something." The eyes of those crowded around the ashcan turned to fishhooks as I crashed their private dinner party. He was so engrossed with a piece of chicken that he didn't even notice me. "Excuse me. I want to ask you something about that song you were singing."

"I just sing the song. I don't explain it," he said, and went back to tearing at his piece of chicken.

I was reminded of the comeback for all forms of explaining in prison: Stop crying and do your time. How you did your time was much more important than why you were doing it. As I heard from men who had more than enough time to think about how they would do it—a man has to have something to do. And when he reaches the point where he feels he has nothing to do, he either dies or he kills.

"What was that all about?" Otis asked when I caught up with him.

"I wanted to ask him about the words to that song but he didn't want to rap."

"Yeah, he don't rap to nobody that ain't in his set . . . Hey, I know this bar we can go to that's right near here. It's called 'Vietnam' and it's owned by some Vietnam vets."

I expected a bar with a name like that to have a particular look or atmosphere. But it didn't. The only thing that struck me about the place was the total absence of women. And the conversation between men seemed to lack the arm-wrestling quality associated with most bar talk.

"So tell me somethin, Mouth."

"There's not much to tell."

"How long were you in the joint?"

"Two years."

"You look like you came out of it all right."

"More or less."

CORNELIUS EADY

CORNELIUS EADY is the author of five books of poetry: *Kartunes* (1980); *Victims of the Last Dance Craze* (1986); *The Gathering of My Name* (1991), nominated for the 1992 Pulitzer Prize in Poetry; and the two forthcoming books *You Don't Miss Your Water* (1995) and *The Autobiography of a Jukebox* (1996). Among various fellowships and awards, Eady is the recipient of an NEA Fellowship in Literature (1985), a John Simon Guggenheim Fellowship in Poetry (1993), and a Rockefeller Foundation Fellowship to Bellagio, Italy (1993). He has taught poetry at Sarah Lawrence College, New York University, the Writer's Voice, and the College of William and Mary. Eady is currently associate professor of English and director of the Poetry Center at SUNY–Stony Brook.

WHEN I AM WRITING POETRY I first look for the music inside of the poem's subject. After I find the music, the next question is how do I stop it from flowing too fast, too long, or in the wrong direction. Usually the poem will tell me.

My poetry is not romantic in the way that it talks about love and loverships. I don't write that kind of poetry. There are very few poems that I write that I would consider "love poems." However, when I am writing a poem about Thelonius Monk or Hank Mobley or John Coltrane—those poems are written *with* love as a sort of declaration to the subject.

In some of my poetry, I describe photographs as a way of appreciating the language in those photographs; the body language, the shading of the light, and the moment in which the photograph was taken. It is not a difficult process because photography and poetry are very similar in that they both encapsulate memories. There is a poem that I wrote about a photograph of Miles Davis. The photo is of Miles Davis playing his horn in the prime of his career in some crowded place in California. I wrote the poem after he had died, and recapturing the moment in his life when the photo had been taken was simply a matter of realizing who and what he was—that boxer's pose, and all of that genius when he played his horn—and then realizing the great loss after his death. The first thing that came to mind was that New York was a slimmer city without him in it—the first line of the poem is: *New York grows/Slimmer/In his absence.*

I see all things in terms of language. I notice things in a room like hand motions, different ongoing conversations, the way the light falls—all of that is in its own way language. So when I'm on the street, I hear the language in, or on, the street. I was walking on the street the other day when I came across two black panhandlers having a conversation. One of them was making sure that the other was all right, asking him if he had had anything to eat. The other said, "Well, yeah, I got a sandwich this morning." With that assurance, the first one said, "Well, fine then, you're good to go!" At that moment, I noticed that there was a younger black kid walking in front of me. He also heard the exchange between the two panhandlers, but it wasn't until he heard "good to go" that he turned around to see what was going on. Because in that phrase— "good to go"—the younger black kid heard the street; he heard his own language and he wanted to find out who was speaking his language. That whole scene that I witnessed on the street could have been a poem, and maybe still will be.

I would like to believe that written language can be universal and accessible to everyone, but I am also aware that it's not. I've always been envious of artists because the medium works so much faster than writing. If you see a painting or an image, it's right there, staring you in the face. If you read a poem, you've got to take it in, think about it, translate it, and then decide whether you like it or not. It is the same with dancing; as an observer, you are interpreting the art simultaneously as you are seeing it—there isn't that lag time that comes when you have to read something through before you are able to get anything from it. That doesn't mean that writers cannot have the same impact as a painter or a dancer, it just means that the writer's readership must entertain some patience.

What I love about writing poetry is that it gives me the ability to take a look at the world; it gives me permission to look at the world through my *own* lenses. I've done a lot of other things, from working on a loading dock to frying hamburgers, and I think that the true blessing of writing is that it provides me with the opportunity to walk around and take in the world at my own speed. I am able to process the world as a writer in a way that I couldn't if I were doing something else.

I forget when I started feeling like a professional writer. It's not really a good idea to get into the insecurities of being a writer—you don't want to go there. I guess I started to *consider* myself a professional writer after the 1980 publication of my first book of poetry, *Kartunes*. I decided at that point that I was committed to being a writer, and that I would carry myself through writing.

The older I get, the more I realize that I am part of a larger tradition, and I really want to talk back and talk within that tradition. I have the sense that as African-American writers we have hardly scratched the surface of who and what we are and how we fit into American culture. I feel that if we don't identify and claim who we are, no one else is going to. I also feel that black culture's idea of "our story" is unchartered territory. We haven't even begun to talk about how the so-called American Experience has really affected us as a race.

My experience as a black writer in America has been that while I may be allowed to speak, I will not be listened to. It's a trick; as black writers, we are told to write our experiences for recognition and respect, and so we write our experiences, but we are then met with hostile or ignorant charges of being too radical or oversensitive about race relations. Why are there no critical works about Langston Hughes's poetry—one of the greatest poets in the twentieth century? Or why can't Amiri Baraka find a publisher who will take on his new work? These two writers have contributed some of the finest writing in the history of black literature. There is something wrong when a culture *chooses* to ignore a large percentage of its writers. African-American writers have been ostracized in America; we have to depend on each other to get the books published, to get the critical evaluations of our work and the exposure of public readings. And that is not because this is the natural order of things.

The experience of being a writer yet not being considered a writer has happened to me and almost every other black writer I know on some level, and it is an experience that needs to be addressed. I feel that it is my responsibility to address that experience. I also want to expand the definition of what an African-American writer is and what an African-American writer can write about. I want the right to define myself and to not be defined by somebody else's idea of what they *think* I should be.

I do not know what the fear is behind the action of taking matters into one's own hands. For black writers it may be difficult to give up the readily available excuse for not doing anything because we don't have the chance—I have heard that from young writers as well as from some of my contemporaries. Black people have grown up with this horrible myth about who we are. We buy into that myth, and sometimes we are not even consciously aware of doing it.

I was talking with Toi Derricotte, a wonderful black woman writer, at the Poetry Society the other night, and she said something very interesting—Toi always says something interesting. She began her portion of the evening's reading by talking about a book she is currently working on called *The Black Notebooks*, which discusses many of the issues surrounding the identity of being black. Toi said that she realized that her conception of what literature is supposed to be came from how she had learned it is supposed to be, and not what it is. She said that she had not read a single black author during the entire time she was in graduate school. Her saying that made me think about the way I conduct my writing workshops sometimes—how I may critique a black poet based on the criteria that I learned while I was in graduate school and, like Toi, not reading black authors; the criteria for what literature is can be one that blocks out the voice, the style, and the identity of black writers.

It is scary to change our perceptions of what we have been taught to believe is good literature. Because basically the action of giving in to change shakes up the structures that we have lived with and have felt safe within. I do have a sense that there is something called "good literature" and that the people who write it don't look like me, don't talk like me, and *don't* come from my neighborhood. So what happens when I decide to throw that sense away? It isn't a matter of simply saying, "Oh well, I'm wise to that now, so I'm going to stop thinking that way." It is a very painful process because I have to realize that the assumptions that I bought may not be exactly what I paid for.

Certainly there is good black literature. That is not really the point. The point that I am trying to make is that there is something called American literature, and then there is something called African-American literature. There is also something called Latino literature, Native American literature, and gay and lesbian literature. Categorizing literatures in this way keeps the "other" at a remove. This action is unquestionably a part of the "big lie" between races in America. It means that African-Americans, as well as other nonwhite cultures, exist in another universe without any interaction with "anybody who counts." I get tired of having to think of literature in these compartments that don't interact with one another.

I am an American writer; I was born here, I grew up here, I'm going to die here—I'm not going to die in Italy, I'm not going to die in Mexico, I'm not going to die in Africa—I'm going to die here, in America. That is who I am, and yet I am not allowed nor given the opportunity to operate in a parallel universe with other Americans. The mistake that we have had in teaching literature is having said, for example, that Richard Wright's *Black Boy* isn't really a novel but an angry testimony that comes from "that side of things"; that there is a canon, and then there are these other books on the sly for a different sort of flavor or perspective.

The exclusion of African-American literature is tremendously damaging to all of us, black and white, because challenging the great mythology of who we are is really what is important. I was thinking of a black novelist during the Harlem Renaissance named Nella Larsen, who if I'm not mistaken was the first black woman writer to win the Guggenheim. Larsen wrote about the interaction between blacks and whites in Harlem. If you go to the magazines of record during that time, there is no mention of her writing. She was known in her era, but when you go back to look for traces of her in the public record, she doesn't show up. That is a tragedy. And the tragedy continues today because we are talking about interactions between other races now, but perhaps that discourse will not show up when somebody tries to look for it in fifty years.

We have been able to make some progress, but I would argue that black writers have laboriously advocated for what little accountability we now have. And even so, there are the last bastions, like the academies, who are talking about "multiculturalism" but still have not really scratched the surface or come up with an honest and a comprehensive treatment of our experience. That bothers me. Now, instead of having nobody of color appear at literary events, we now have "special nights"—like "special-needs children." We are constantly surrounded by this reality; we are in, but we are not in; we are allowed to talk, but no one is really listening. Historically, we have tried to negotiate with this reality;

now I think it is time for us to create another reality. We need to make a statement of our own and say: "All the rest of y'all can come if you want, but if you don't, we're doing it anyway."

In making a clear break from the definitions that have been put upon us, we release some of the pain of racism and the history of our enslaved people. It is very difficult because letting the pain go does not mean that we will not be reminded of the reality at every turn. This makes me think of something that Toni Morrison wrote in *Beloved* about all the different ways in which black people try to get over, get around, and get through our slave history, and yet it is still there. Morrison was saying, "What does it take?" I can't think of the exact quote, but it was to the effect that we try this, we try that, and we still have to deal with it. I feel that letting go of the pain is not letting go of the reality of racism, but rather an attempt to reinvent who we are and how *we* choose to feel about certain things.

I definitely don't want to make this all sound negative. Don't get me wrong, I love being a black writer. If there was a magic potion that I could take that would make me into a white writer, I wouldn't take it. I think my position as a writer in black culture gives me a perspective that I wouldn't get anywhere else; I get to know things about this country that I wouldn't get to know any other way. If we let it, writing gives us crucial information about ourselves. Being a black writer gives me a unique rite of passage that I feel grateful to have.

It is difficult to find strategies that will place my history in a healthy perspective while at the same time trying to flourish as a writer. But when all of the conflicts and definitions are stripped away, I am a writer. My basic instinct tells me that I am a writer, and I will continue to interact with the words and the rest of the world whether it is recognized, recorded, or remembered.

From
THE AUTOBIOGRAPHY
OF A JUKEBOX
Papa Was a Rolling Stone

A few weeks before my father died, my sister tells me a fuzzy story about a young woman she'd heard rumors about, a class or two ahead of her in high school, who carried our unusual last name.

And when my niece goes through some of my father's papers, she uncovers a small, laminated card, a birth certificate from a midwestern state, for a boy, born a year before I was, though it's a different last name.

What about this? We want to know, and we badger my father in the hospital, until he finally admits to us that the woman my sister tried, but never got to meet in high school was indeed our half-sister.

My father tells us that when my niece was an infant, and my sister was living away in Florida, he'd bundle my niece up and take her to this woman's apartment. He was that proud of being a grand-father, and he knew my niece would be too young to remember.

She married a rich man, and they moved away to Israel, is as far as he's willing to take us on this. *She's happy, and I don't want to bother her.*

And the birth certificate? I see language in the way the bones in his thin body twist; his mouth says, *beats me.*

He's pissed-off that it's come down to this, that his children would have enough time to try and unravel a man's business.

And then he clucked, which I took to mean, *what makes you think I owe you this?*

Photo of Miles Davis at Lennies-on-the-Turnpike, 1968

New York grows
Slimmer
In his absence.
I suppose

You could also title this picture
Of Miles, his leathery
Squint, the grace
In his fingers *a sliver of the stuff*

You can't get anymore,
As the rest of us wonder:
What was the name
Of driver

Of that truck? And the rest
Of us sigh:
Death is one hell
Of a pickpocket.

Tramp

I need a haircut, but this guy clearly doesn't understand what's on my head. I become nervous when I see a blank stare as I try to explain to him what a slow fade is.

What can I say about the history of my hair? Once, I had a poetry manuscript which had the word *nappy* mixed somewhere in its title; once, I wore different floppy hats; once, you could set my blood to boil simply by pulling an afro pick from out of a back pocket, rake a soft "do" as if God played fashion favorites.

In high school in the late sixties, weren't our afros mythical? Didn't George Jackson die because some guards believed his hair was capable of storage, little bush of anger, tiny grove of long, hidden blades?

How many times did my family think a proper haircut would put my feet on the right path, set my mind straight? Once, my father got a cousin who was a back-alley barber to "relax" my hair. When he was finished with the uneven lye, and before he cut it, I was able to look in a shard of mirror, see that my hair happened to be longer than my mother's, all that wound-up energy given permission to roll, to blow in a breeze.

I was so pissed-off by this "cure," that I let it go to hell, let it tangle into long, vengeful dreads I wasn't to cut until I began teaching college, and only then because the school was down south.

Some friends innocently recommended this new hairplace, just a few blocks from my house. The barber's friendly, and game, but he's up against home-boy hair, urban steel wool, industrial-strength kink.

We both act as if we're on a bad blind date, well-intentioned, but soon forgotten. I leave forty dollars lighter, a few snips cleaner, and carrying a memory of one of my dear aunts, who didn't know what to make of this mess either.

I'll Fly Away

O, young black American teenaged boy-child, I
know what runs through your head
    In Venice at the bridge at Academia. A bit of
lire has slipped from your pocket,
    A young, white foreign woman has seen this,
picks it up, and calls
    for your attention. Your cautious response
Is more than a difference of tongues.
    Your body tenses; a traditional brace
for the blues.

    She is smiling and tries to hand
Your money back. A bit of you is
    still back in the States,
Where a simple exchange like this
    sometimes hides a stiff reminder.
Clearly, my brother, this isn't the world

    We come from. In mid-day Venice
You move towards her outstretched arm
    a little slower than shy,
As if you'll have need of a sober witness,
    as if this is where you know
The experiment ends, and memory dogs
    'round the corner.

TREY ELLIS

TREY ELLIS is the author of two novels and several screenplays. He is still and often best identified by his groundbreaking essay titled "The New Black Aesthetic," which was published in the black literary journal *Callaloo* in 1990. His novels are *Platitudes* (1988) and *Home Repairs* (1993). He lives with his wife in Santa Monica, California.

WHEN I WAS A KID I envisioned writers as being these really cool guys who lived on sailboats and typed into the night under the stars. It seemed like it would be a great life. And it has been.

I have written about funny or satirical themes from the very beginning. I never thought about writing any other way. Being funny or finding the humor in something comes very easy to me. I am only somewhat aware of trying to be funny when I am writing a story, and sometimes it feels like a concerted effort. I know that I am doing it right if I am laughing myself. Observational humor, and really any sort of humor, is such an important aspect of life.

What is funniest to me is looking at and laughing at the things that are really screwed up in this world. I don't believe in sacred cows. I take one of those screwed-up things and try to satirically push it to its logical and ludicrous conclusion in order to make the point that this thing that we may think is weird is actually very, very weird. Like the "Jackson Family Reunion" that was on TV— if you look at it, it's weird; but if you really look at it, it's *really* weird. Not much is not funny to me. I even like Howard Stern when he's not talking about black people.

I think that humor is intellectually challenging. There is no shame in being a humorist, although it is never given the same respect as the more serious and critical literature. I have certainly found that to be so with my first two novels, *Platitudes* and *Home Repairs*. I feel that if they were more serious, they would be taken more seriously, which is too bad. I haven't found most book reviewers to have a terrific sense of humor, though. It seems that when book reviewers come across a comic novel, they immediately think the writer just dashed it off the top of his or her head. That is their failing, not mine. Woody Allen once likened moving from comedy films to dramatic films to moving from the children's table to the adults' table, which I totally disagree with. I think that as a comic writer in any medium, you need to stand behind your guns and not feel ashamed for having a strong and intelligent sense of humor.

There wasn't an overabundance of joking at the family table when I was a kid; my parents fought a lot, my sister and I fought a lot—there was a lot of tension. Perhaps forming a sense of humor was my defense against the sort of tumultuous atmosphere in my home growing up—it wasn't an unhappy home, just crazy.

I have always taken my writing to heart. At one time I had thought that I would become an engineer or an astronomer so that I could make a living, and that I would start writing books after I had retired. My mother died when I was sixteen, which made me realize that you can't really make long-term plans. So I figured that if I wanted to be a writer, I'd better do it. I burned my bridges on purpose and consequently had no skill other than writing.

I started writing *Platitudes* while I was at Stanford. Instead of writing the series of short stories that I had been assigned to write in my fiction course, I started writing a novel. After I graduated from college, with the novel unfinished, I tried to get jobs writing for comedy television shows like "Saturday Night Live" and "Not Necessarily the News," a satire on HBO at the time. I didn't get hired anywhere, so I moved to Italy, where I had spent my junior year. In Florence, I taught English, sold sporting goods, was a weight-training instructor, acted a little bit, modeled a little bit, and finished the novel. I strapped myself to a chair and wrote for four hours every morning in order to finish the book. I had a clock next to my elbow as I was writing—I would start at eight o'clock and wasn't allowed to get up until twelve o'clock.

The odd jobs that I was doing to pay my rent were monotonous and distracting, but they also made me write harder and faster. It was a lot like what I imagine long-distance running would be like. I didn't start out writing for four hours each morning when I first began the process. I started at one hour, then two, then finally working my way up to four hours. The reason I picked four hours is because I had read interviews with writers in *The Paris Review*, and they said that they wrote for about four hours each day. It was hard, though. I would like to devise a writer's chair with a time-release seat belt on it—you wouldn't be able to get up out of the chair until you had written for a certain amount of time.

My ambition to be a novelist was what ultimately provided the necessary discipline required to finish writing *Platitudes*. I knew that if I didn't write, I would never become a novelist. I had worked as a freelance journalist at *Newsweek* the summer before I moved to Italy, and had met a lot of very good journalists who would tell me after I told them I wanted to be a novelist, "Oh yeah, I've got a novel—fifty pages there, two hundred here, not finished, but I keep dabbling at it." I didn't want to be like that. I didn't want to live with the regret I heard in the voices of those journalists.

I finished writing the novel after I had been in Italy for about eight months. I gave the completed manuscript to a friend to bring back to the States and went to travel in Africa for four months. I guess at that point I didn't think that I was going to publish the book. I had once heard a rather well-known writer say, "You should write a book, stick it in a drawer, pick it up ten years later, and then you will know what is good and what is bad about it." When I had finally finished the novel, I actually thought that I would go back to *Newsweek* and work as a foreign correspondent for a while and then later on I would pick the novel back up. It really didn't occur to me that it would get published. Being a novelist meant writing a novel, and I had done that.

I moved to New York after returning to the States. I had written the novel in longhand in a series of notebooks, so I typed it up on an old Smith Corona typewriter. I wanted to get some feedback on the book, and a friend of mine at *Newsweek*, Dennis Williams, told me to send the manuscript to his father, John A. Williams *(The Man Who Cried I Am)*. Williams really liked it, and he gave me Ishmael Reed's address, and so I sent it to Ishmael Reed. Both Williams and Reed gave me advance quotes for the back of the book, and that is when I began to imagine that the book might become a real book.

I got an agent after about a year of trying, and he shopped the manuscript around for another year or so after that until it was finally sold and then published. It felt great to have the book published, but I had expected a different lifestyle to come along with its publication. *Platitudes* came out in the Vintage Contemporary line, and I had read about other authors in the same series, like Jay McInerney, who were living these high-style lives, dating models, and going to great parties. Right after the book had been published, my editor invited me out to lunch. I thought we were going to go to the Quilted Giraffe or some really nice place in New York. I didn't have any nice clothes, so I borrowed some. When I got to my editor's office he asked me why I was so dressed up. We ate at a little dive of a sushi bar around the corner.

Even after the book was published, I still couldn't survive as a freelance journalist. I was proofreading at *Rolling Stone* magazine. I had written a book and no one would hire me! It was very frustrating. When I decided to become a writer I knew the danger involved, I knew that it was a real crapshoot. But I also knew that I didn't want to be some aging and embittered fifty-year-old proofreader. I took the risk head-on. Writing is a matter of courage and confidence, but it is also a matter of sensibility and drive. Hemingway said that every writer needs a good "bullshit detector," and if you don't have one you could still have the drive to write, and could keep driving and driving, but never get anywhere. Some days I think I'm not a good writer, other days I think I'm going to be the youngest novelist to win the Pulitzer Prize, but I always have the drive to write and the sensibility to know that it is absolutely what I want to do.

The idea of *Platitudes* just came to me. I first thought of a young boy lying facedown in a field thinking about life. I started writing with this character and really liked him, but the tone became boring to me after a while. Then I heard this other voice, Isshee, the feminist author, and she came into my mind critiquing the first, sexist author. It just felt right to have them alternately narrating the story. I really wrote the book as it went along. I had no idea what it was going to be about until it was written.

Writing from the perspective of the young boy was not that difficult, but later on, writing from the perspective of a young girl was more challenging and lots of fun. The female protagonist in *Platitudes* was based loosely on my cousin and her group of girlfriends. My cousin went to a private high school in New York, and she would tell me all of these incredible stories about the experiences she had with her girlfriends. They created this great language that was sort of a cross between Valley Girl talk and street talk. So I wanted to include that language and the girls who created it in the book.

The writing process was a little different with my second book, *Home Repairs*, because I began the story with the idea that I would write a fictional autobiography. I was older than the protagonist when I began writing it, so I was looking back at my own life, at my family, and at my friends. By fictional autobiography I mean that I wanted to write a confessional book that was not necessarily about my life but that felt real and that was told in the first person. I wanted the book to read as though the protagonist was spilling his most closely guarded secrets. I felt that writing it in a diary format was the best way to convey that effect because a diary is the only place where our discourse is honest. When we talk to other people, we might say certain things because we are flirting with someone, or because we are trying to impress someone, like a boss or a teacher, but when you are alone talking to your diary, it's like talking to your psychiatrist. Unless you know it's going to be published, which is why the conceit of the book, although I didn't spell it out, was that the diary had been found by someone else and then published.

I put on a hat when I am writing from the perspective of any of the characters in my work. I put on the hat of each character and start talking like him or her, as if I were possessed by his or her personality. It's like speaking in tongues. The first-person passages in *Platitudes* were written as fast as I could spit them out, almost in one draft.

There are a lot of different kinds of writing in *Platitudes*, which may be confusing to some readers, but the book is about clichés in writing, so I consciously used as many different styles and mediums as I could. I wanted to talk about different conventions in writing and the various genres between experimental fiction and the more conventional southern black writing. I like reading interesting and difficult books. I wrote a book that I wanted to read.

The experience of a black middle-class kid who is sort of nerdy and not very self-confident, growing up in the suburbs, which is the subject matter in both *Platitudes* and *Home Repairs*, is such virginal territory in black literature that it was hard to imagine what my readership or audience might be. Whereas in white literature you find that same experience but through the eyes of a white middle-class kid everywhere. But I have found the largest response to be from young adults, both white and black, between the ages of maybe eighteen and thirty.

Because I am black, my writing is filtered through a black sensibility. Neither of my two books are political per se, but by virtue of the fact that the characters are black middle-class figures who have rarely been presented in fiction, the books become political. We watch television, movies, and we read books, yet we rarely see someone on the screen or on the page who is looking back at us with our same eyes. What I think is most important about both of my books is that they give voice to millions of black people who have been historically voiceless.

I am intensely political, and because my novels are not pointedly political, I need an outlet for my politics. So I write Op-Ed pieces and a lot of essays. Eventually I'd like to publish a collection of essays. My family was heavily Democratic, and I have always been fairly leftist. Obviously the "plight of black America" is something that I write about and that most black people talk about daily. I also think and write about the politics in South Africa a lot. I am concerned with the world's cowardice that manifests in all sorts of terrible realities at an all-too rapid pace. I really believe that everyone needs to be much more of an activist in order to create change.

The state of affairs within the black community, from gangsta rap to black-on-black violence, is insane. We are losing our spiritual core—society is beating it out of us with the never-ending institutionalized racism in this country. After all of these years we have been able to withstand it, to still stand up strong, and to search for higher ground. Up until now, we have always been so sure that no matter what was happening to us, we were morally superior to anyone else because slavery and the blatant residual racism was and is so evil. But we are losing that high ground, and it is especially apparent in the things that young black men are saying and doing to young black women. In her book *Of Mules and Men*, Zora Neale Hurston talks about black life that certainly included violence and people getting shot. I am aware that black-on-black violence is timeless and omnipresent. But I don't think that it has ever started so young and been so pervasive as now.

Although I was raised in white neighborhoods, I was also raised by two strong black parents. We always had books like Eldridge Cleaver's *Soul on Ice* and poetry by Nikki Giovanni; we celebrated Kwanzaa; there were a lot of African sculptures and other black art around our house. My sister and I were drenched in positive blackness. I recognize the difference between my experience as a youth and that of many young black kids today. I hope that I have the strength and the skills to help reestablish our spiritual core. Writing is only one of the many ways to begin.

From
PLATITUDES

Dorothy steps from the train at 125th and looks across the girders and tracks to the far token booth and her godfather inside. SWEET DREAMS, DARLING, he says into his microphone, but due to faulty wiring she hears BLEERT DORPSCHTICK. She blows him a kiss, then walks quickly—head ballerina-rigid—across nearly still Lenox Avenue to Fifth Avenue and her apartment building. During her first year at private school, when she was ten, she told the other students just that she lived on upper Fifth Avenue. Before unlocking her building's outer door, she makes sure the light inside is on. If it is dark in the hallway, she either waits to enter with another tenant or for a squad car to pass. She opens the elevator door, waits for its inner door to automatically scrape open, presses 3, and waits for the hum and the upward jerk. Unlocking her front door locks, she enters and relocks the door. The velour couch is still shrink-wrapped with thick, clear vinyl. The mantel over the plastic logs and red light-bulb fire still supports the graduation picture of her big sister. Shawniqua's head leans over a shoulder as if the Yale mortarboard were too heavy a weight. Next to the gilded frame a note from her mother tells her that Aunt Nadine is sick again so Darcelle will be nursing her all night. Dorothy presses the glass face of the new, black, remote-control television. It is still warm.

I know y'all's up, so don't even try to hide it.

In her brothers' room, she hears bodies sliding between sheets. She opens the twins' door to see Don and Vaughn lying in their beds, their eyelids closed so tightly they wrinkle. She kisses them both on the cheeks. The twins each rub at the spots.

Night, you cute little fakers, and in the morning remember to leave me some corn flakes.

She closes the door triumphantly (*clickk*). Giggles bubble from the joyous room.

In her own room she steps down from her red pumps and drives them into the closet with a kick. She unzips the bottom of her peg-leg jeans, unbuckles the belt, and inhales to slip her thumbs inside the waistband to unbutton the top button, then pops out the other four buttons. By bending one leg, then the other leg, she rotates her bottom out of the pant seat. Then it's one last firm push over the thighs, and the jeans slouch dead to the floor.

The blouse she unbuttons before the mirror, turning to watch the light smear and shine over the silk over her breasts, the deep-brown mounds revealed slowly as her nipples extend hydraulically. She turns to see how her panties curve with her hip and how—by rising on point and flexing her bottom—each buttock becomes a ball. She fingers the light switch down (Off) with her free hand.

December 26, 1984

Dear Sir:

I must now confess that your writing challenges me. Though you persist in this suicidal and unforgivable penchant for pornography, I must admit that this latest passage on Dorothy is not altogether without merit. The dialectic between class struggle and cultural assimilation, the mental anguish of rising (???!) from a middle-class Harlem household to the rich, white, New York, controlled-substance-abusing elite is almost interestingly handled. Of course you then proceed to ruin it all with more misogynistic belches, where women control every eroto-romantic encounter—always to the detriment of the male. It is this naive, wrongheaded, and backward assessment of life that will continue to fetter your lofty literary aspirations.

As for the "joyous room" crack on page 108, this cynical swipe at my prose style (very successful and oft-awarded, I might remind you) was not as vicious as your having had me killed with that frying pan—truly a low point in this very rough draft. Are you finally beginning to heed my earnest and well-meant advice? It is gratifying to see, finally, the tempering of your excruciatingly nomadic prose style.

About *my* contribution to your novel. True, I began these consultations without an eye toward the publication of my own segments, yet I would be less than honest were I not to admit that my editor has expressed an interest in the piece. Of course you will be remunerated for the use of your characters' names, so fear not. My lawyer is drawing up the contract.

I also know the director of a black advertising firm there in New York. Perhaps your talents could be more lucratively exploited as a copywriter. I have already given her your address, so you should be hearing from Gloria at the start of the new year.

With the utmost sincerity,
Isshee Ayam

P.S. I truly wish you and yours a most merry Kwanzaa and a Happy New Year.

P.P.S. Your stand on negritude, sir, continues to befuddle me, and I would be interested, and perhaps the authorities would also be interested, in knowing if your apartment looks onto a certain Italian dance studio.

12/31/84

Dear Ms. Ayam,

I usually do not write personal letters while still on a book's first draft, but your letter of the twenty-sixth prompted this swift response.

You are absolutely correct. My prose and my thoughts have changed, tightened, and—if I may be so bold—improved. Isshee—may I call you that—for after just having read and thoroughly enjoyed your *Chillun o' de Lawd*, *Hog Jowl Junction*, and *My Big Ol' Feets Gon' Stomp Dat Evil Down*, I feel a real intimacy between us; even though you can know only my latest piece. Unfortunately, my major work, *Hackneyed*, is still only available in manuscript form and, at that, only in precious few "serious" bookstores.

More on *Platitudes*. I feel I must explain myself, and forgive me if I am more confiding now than our past, adversarial relationship had allowed. Last year, after an ugly incident too complicated and sordid (and a story as old as those of noble Chaucer) to detail, my wife left me. Not only was I emotionally devastated, but she—as a well-connected matriarch of the black New York bourgeoisie—stranded me from all financially advantageous situations in this city. Needless to say, it has been a very lean year. Consequently, I am afraid the stress of my "real life," especially during this, my first holiday season alone, has invaded my narrative. An unforgivable occurrence professionally, I am sure, but nonetheless an all-too-human one. If I should again stumble, please understand.

I am sure you are aware that on February 20, 21, and 22 at the Wellesley Hotel here in New York, the annual BAA conference will take place. I have always shied away from black author anythings, because I find them both pompous and aggrandizing, and controlled by hacks and phonies like that Afro-Florentine expatriate sham Richard Johnson (who is Dorothy's male-model friend's namesake, by the way). However, if you are planning to attend, I would be delighted to meet you face to face.

Oh, and thank you for the job recommendation; however, I am afraid that for now at least I am committed to the full-time lifestyle of the starving artist. Yet if *Platitudes* never does find a kindly publishing house, I might very well be calling your friend.

In New York I can be reached at (212) 719-9800. If for any reason a recorded message tells you the number has been disconnected, do not be alarmed. I am currently having a rather trivial dispute with the phone company that I am confident of resolving shortly.

Your colleague and fan,
Dewayne

P.S. As for your publishing your version of *Platitudes*, please do not do anything rash. In my current state, I cannot protest too loudly, yet I am confident that we will be able to work something out.

P. P. S. I have often wondered why you never allow your picture on the inside cover of your books, so have been curious to associate a face with your stirring prose. A very short while ago I discovered your splendid interview in *Newsweek* magazine and was very pleasantly surprised to find color photographs of you at home and attending your aerobics/self-defense class. Not to be overly obsequious, but you have nothing to be embarrassed about. At all.

Still, to correct my unfair advantage, enclosed is a fairly recent photograph of the "real" me.

LEON FORREST

LEON FORREST was born on January 8, 1937, in Chicago, Illinois. He was educated at Wilson Junior College, Roosevelt University, and the University of Chicago. He is the author of four novels: *There Is a Tree More Ancient Than Eden* (1973); *The Bloodsworth Orphans* (1977); *Two Wings to Veil My Face* (1984), which won the DuSable Museum Certificate of Merit and Achievement for Fiction, the Carl Sandburg Award, the Friends of Literature Prize, and the Society of Midland Authors Award for Fiction; and *Divine Days* (1992/1993), which won the *Chicago Sun-Times* Book-of-the-Year Award for Fiction in 1992. Forrest's collection of essays, *Relocations of the Spirit,* was published in 1994. He has been a professor of African-American Studies and English at Northwestern University since 1973 and has chaired the Department of African-American Studies since 1985.

BEYOND THE HARD WORK and discipline, no one knows what makes the magic of writing.

I've been around a long time as a writer. My writing is difficult to get at; it is a difficult style. Most readers want an immediate plot and an immediate narrative, and sometimes with my work the reader has to wait a couple hundred pages before the plot or narrative is fully revealed. I never think about changing my style of writing. Lord, no! A singer couldn't change the way he sang, even if he were asked. My writing is the way I sing. I wouldn't dare change it. A writer must be bullheaded about his or her own view of life and the ways in which he or she expresses that view.

I came from a very ambitious family that was more concerned about my actually doing something with my life than the fact that I had chosen writing as what I would do. Initially I had wanted to write poetry, and of course my mother asked me how I was going to eat if I was a poet. But my parents loved to read. My mother used to read to me. And my father, who was a railroad bartender, would read to us when he was home. Reading used to mean a lot more in lower-middle-class America before the real onslaught of television than it does now.

I showed some of my writing to a professor I had in college and asked him if he thought I had any promise. He told me that I did have some talent but, more importantly, that I should go out and try to be a writer because I would always be miserable if I didn't. When I started to take the idea of being a writer seriously, it felt like somewhat of a religious experience. Beyond the romantic part of finding my voice through writing, it was the willfullness, the sense of mission, and the power of the discipline that took me over in such a way that I knew I had to surrender my life to it. I would never have predicted such power from the written word.

The intellectual demands of writing are very strong because ultimately any good writer is a thinker. When I initially started writing I seemed to have a certain gift of facility for the immediacy of language, but I didn't know if I would be able to match that gift with a mature enough intellect. It was a matter of going from a certain emotion that drove me to write, to the development of my mind and my spirit. And that development formed in me what might be called a "writer's mind," which is highly reflective and deeply associative; always making patterns of thinking. This process of development required a very strict discipline of reading, and an ability then to transform what I read into creative craftsmanship using original material.

The patterns of thinking in writing are also patterns of narrative, of philosophical and spiritual heritage, of my relationship with oral tradition and literary tradition, and then the relationship between the two traditions themselves. One of the things that I admire about writers like Ralph Ellison and Toni Morrison is their ability to make that relationship between oral and literary tradition into such a lovely and exhilarating fabric. But reading is more important than anything else. Because if you just live, even though you may experience enough of life for yourself, it might not be enough of an experience to really learn and understand human compassion. Listening to people and watching the way they laugh, the way they behave and move around in society is very natural, and it is a good way to learn about other people's lives. What isn't natural is learning how to read in a way that teaches technique.

Being a writer requires a tremendous amount of patience; patience in developing narrative, patience in one's own private life and the ability to put selfish and personal things on hold. And then, of course, the patience with writing itself—the last of all of the disciplines to develop within the individual writer. One must also develop a sense of the importance of the isolation and loneliness of writing. Writing is the most lonely of all the trades. It is not like being in a dance troupe where if somebody falls ill, then somebody else can pick up the slack. There is no one other than the writer himself who is able to pick up where he left off. Writing is really very secretive and private.

The ability to work alone in complete solitude is difficult. I remember when I first got the notion of writing in my head, I set up my typewriter at the beach thinking that I would be able to write while I socialized and looked at young ladies! But this is not the way of the writer. The solitude and the loneliness are the dues that a writer must pay. The writer must take everything he or she needs from the beauty parlor, the barbershop, or the town bar and then go home into some small room and re-create those scenes through memory, imagination, and discipline. Building a tolerance for that loneliness is difficult if you are a young writer, which may well be one of the reasons why most writers develop later in life—it takes a certain strength and wisdom of character.

What kept me committed to building that tolerance as a young writer was that I could do things at the typewriter that I could never do in public debate or argument. I was always the last person to come up with a witty line. I knew I could find that witty line if only I were in front of a typewriter. I think sometimes people who are very good oral storytellers are often so taken with their voices and their audiences that they are not able to convey the same stories through writing. It is a different kind of rhythm. The person at the party who sits at the piano with everyone crowded around him may be able to play a song to the note if he is given the first few lines to work with, but that same person might not be able to compose an original piece of music.

Ultimately, the reader will feel most deeply about the writer's work in his or her own solitude. The rich relationship between a writer and his reader is one on one. While it may be delightful to hear a writer such as Toni Morrison read her work out loud, at the same time the deepest appreciation will come from reading her work over and over again. So there is a pattern created between the reader and the writer as well. The writer writes in solitude and the reader reads in solitude. Maybe that's why some of the best writing comes out of prisons.

Another thing about the aspect of loneliness and solitude in writing is that oftentimes when a writer becomes very famous he sheds his loneliness and his work deteriorates as he becomes a public figure. If a well-known writer came into a bar full of people, the customers would all say, "Oh, isn't that so and so!" having more of an interest in the writer's fame than in his talent, which can have a bad effect on any artist but particularly on a writer because the attention can get at the strength of the writer's inner world, making him feel more important than the writing he does. I myself am an enormously mediocre person in every conceivable way. But what I can do with written material is, in some instances, fairly remarkable.

It is very dangerous when a writer starts looking at himself as equally important to his writing. Of course we are all individually important to the people who love us, but it is damaging if the writer takes himself more seriously than his work. The wonderful and imaginative world of the writer is quite different from the writer himself being wonderful and imaginative. It may well be that Hemingway might also be a great hunter and fisherman in addition to being a great writer, as his writing might imply, but if

Hemingway were to have thought that he was more important as a public figure, then the interior of his work would not be what it was and is today.

Writing is really quite fragile; it is a remarkable cluster of words and design. Even though a writer must have an enormous ego, he must also have a certain amount of humility. At any given time when I am writing, I generally feel as though the words that I am writing have been given to me by some unknown force, and that I must approach them with a combination of great confidence and great insecurity—two senses that must always be present in a writer's mind. One day I fear I can't do it, the next day I fear I can. When a writer submits to the priesthood of writing, there are things that he simply *must* do, and there is no point in questioning them. For instance, if I am not willing to assume all of the responsibilities that come along with writing—which often stem from the naturally chaotic demands of creativity—then I'd better quit. Further, I must maintain a certain leverage over the chaos of my own creativity, or I will destroy myself.

I was attracted to the idea of teaching on the college level because all of the writers I admired were also teaching, and because I was at the point where I felt that teaching was the next stage of development for me. I felt that I would be able to grow intellectually in a university atmosphere. I had been working in journalism for quite a while and had reached my cutoff point. I knew a lot of people who wanted to talk about gossip but not that many people who wanted to talk about books.

I don't teach creative writing, I prefer to teach literature. It is a wonderful challenge to try and convey the appreciation of literature to my students, which can be very hard because of all of the distractions for young people today. But it is very important that I keep trying because as a writer it is my responsibility to my students, the next generation, to try to convey that the rich complexity of the human experience is best manifested in literature. But it is an uphill battle because of television, VCRs, deconstructionism—all of these factors that water down the sacredness of the literary text.

I don't really separate my connection to Western culture from black literature. I feel as though certainly many of the great writers such as Ellison have been influenced by the tradition of Western culture. Issues of race, class, and oral tradition connect me to Faulkner, Hemingway, and also to Gabriel Garcia Marquez. For example, I am fascinated by the whole issue of turning the horror of suffering into art that I have come to find more poignant and passionate in Russian literature than in any other literature. All of these influences are part of my literary heritage. So on some levels I don't like to look at traditions and cultures in a segregated manner. Even though I may always want to go to a black barbershop, my reading mind must always be open.

Recently, there was an interview with me in *The New Yorker* on Ralph Ellison. I talked about how in black culture if it is a young lady's birthday, we would probably give her one of Toni Morrison's books, whereas if it is a male adolescent's birthday, we would tend to give him a pair of tickets to see a Bulls' basketball game. We don't make intellectual demands of our young black men. We also have lost control of the streets in the lower levels of society, which in many ways prevents me personally from getting to young black men. I have reached the level of intellectual and spiritual peace of mind that I have through books, but that doesn't mean much of anything to the young black men who are selling drugs in the street. If I don't have an immediate power in the economy that these young people are involved in, then I can't get to them. What can I say when one of these young people asks me how much I make writing books?

It is wonderful what black men have accomplished in sports. I have a great deal of respect for athletes. But of late, the price of that accomplishment has been the denigration of the life of the mind. Certainly we all contribute to this—we all think that Michael Jordan is immortal. However, we must begin to bring back currency to the life of the mind in order to exist in the twenty-first century. I think there was a time when education was held in high regard. The civil rights movement demonstrated the value of education and discipline with its marches and protests. Those marches showed intelligence and honored the life of the mind. Everyone was and is very interested in how Malcolm X was able to tell white folks off so well, but nobody talks about the books he read. We need to focus on how, through reading, he was able to transform himself from the worst kind of human being to a human being with very constructive and intelligent attributes.

There is a feeling that I get from writing that I sort of blow on like a flame; the heat reaches other people so that it is not only generating my heartbeat, but it is generating the reader's heartbeat too. Writing is all I have. It has been my special luck to have this talent, and I have never thought about doing anything else. I use the system of writing up to a point of ecstasy or exhaustion, and then I'll stop so that I have something to start on the next day.

From

DIVINE DAYS

WEDNESDAY, FEBRUARY 16, 1966, 6:00 A.M.

Last night I returned to Forest County from a two-year stint in the Army. I've made certain concrete demands upon my soul, in order to take over my life, so that I can regiment my emotional waywardness, and my easily distracted intellect, mainly to shape out my dreams of becoming a major playwright. I've even mentally mapped out my schedule for the first seven days. If I can hold to my plan, generate a regular journal, and then use it as a springboard for my dramatic ventures, I'll be on my way to fulfilling my quest.

My beloved Aunt Eloise believes that keeping a journal will help me in this "avocational" endeavor (she also thinks that this "exercise" will exorcise the playwright out of my soul; I'll be so overwhelmed, so daunted that I'll content myself with simply becoming a feature story writing journalist).

Dear Aunt Eloise who raised me after my mother (her younger sister, Agnes) was killed in a plane crash when I was three, who a short time later married my father, who is both my aunt and my stepmother . . . who married her current husband, Hugh High Hickles (a man twenty-five years her senior), a decade after daddy's (violent) death (I was "orphaned" thus a week shy of my twelfth birthday).

Three weeks ago, Aunt Eloise wired me in Germany, concerning the death of Sugar-Groove, that mythic soul of Forest County, whose early memory was forged mainly in Mississippi. It is his stories, founded upon these memories, that I feel destined to dramatize. During the course of transforming his life, I personally hope to discover a meaning of existence out of this man's divine days upon this planet. Yet to many, Sugar-Groove's life appeared so hapless. Aunt Eloise often called Sugar-Groove "a winging waif—an eternal wunderkind." I could not accept the report of Sugar-Groove's death, at first, given the mystery surrounding his last days upon this earth, and my continual wonderment—down the years—at Sugar-Groove's capacity for self-regeneration. I had heard the spectacular voice of his enchanting soul, so clearly alive and enunciating within my mind. I've wanted to write a play about the soul within the voice of Sugar-Groove. But that would be as difficult as my failed experiment (born out of a dream) of trying to run a ladder up the hieroglyphics of Charlie Parker's tortured soul, then transforming this experience of his voice into a one-act play. I even took saxophone lessons in an attempt to get back to the pure madness of his voice, attempting imitative solos in the basement of my Aunt's tavern, while listening to Bird's flights of fancy on my small record player. I am afraid, alas, that the passionate remains of "Bird Lives" will never know two boards, nor arise from the bottom of my instrument case in the basement of Aunt Eloise's Night Light Lounge (next to the wall where we keep the beer cases) and in the exact place where W.A.D. Ford's mammoth canine ALL SOULS dwelt once upon a time.

I wrote a play about this trickster W.A.D. Ford and sent it off last year when I came home from Germany on a month's leave. I've yet to hear from the seven theatrical companies (I did have a strong contact with The Raven Players) concerning my attempt to capture Ford's voice within his soul. When you meet Ford you may argue that he is without a soul. I say *is* because, although he disappeared, that serial hermaphrodite has hardly tasted death.

I've been hearing voices all of my life (among my earliest memories are those echoing words of Aunt Eloise's pure soprano bird voice singing, "Twinkle, Twinkle little star, how I wonder what you are") since before I can remember. Sometimes these incantations overtake me, speaking not only to me, but through me and rendering me up frazzled and daffy. My face becomes the mask for their mean-hearted merriment. Or there are those voices, like that of Hans Henson, which swirl up from the pit of my soul, out of the immediate and living, earthly guts of real-life experience. They can drive me up the wall of madness, or into a paralysis of inaction.

Great character actors, I believe, often have a certain facial quality—the rubbery mask of a countenance that can produce a cast of a thousand faces. There are others too who can do imitations of voices so well that they hear a voice within the character and then proceed to pitch and project the very soul of that voice out of the character, onto the stage. They actually craft a stage voice. Or should I say that they stage a voice? Others unleash many voices through the roles they play. Their own layers—all in readiness—awaken from the playwright's palette of a thousand grease-painted, sweaty soul-faces, as he sketches away. For they (the characters' voices) lived within the playwright before they were born upon the stage, or the canvas.

I have an awful memory for faces, but an excellent one for voices. I'm always getting people who look something alike confused (take Noah Ridgerook Grandberry and Ford, but that's another story, I shall tell later). I'm too hypersensitively attuned to the sound of voices, babblings, other-worldly and worldly tongues. I never forget the nuances of sounds within voices. Sometimes my imitation of voices—as a kind of avocation—can delight a party and for a long time my so-called gift was in demand. I also read palms. A good way to get a pretty girl onto your lap, for starters. The plague of inner voices so riddled me—because you see I have no control over those moments when these voices, or a specific voice, might hit me, or what he'll say, or what she might demand of me. I had to stop doing these imitations, lest they unleash certain spirits from within. I now rely completely on my palm-reading powers for social entree. For when a voice hits me, I'm like a man caught up in a shooting gallery. Yet on a few occasions, I've benefitted directly by hearing the right jamming voice, within a lackluster, unmovable situation.

Not reverie, nor nostalgia, nor melancholia, nor that most mis-used term, déjà vu, none of these explain from where the voices within me hail. In certain cases I've assigned these voices surnames. Names as concepts, over-lines to captions for voices that appear when I dream, awake or sleeping. These coinages aren't as original as my long-gone friend Sugar-Groove's many nicknames, but some of the names I identify regularly are Stranger, Friend, Wrangler, Dr. Duplicity, Connie Dixon Rivers, Mary Mongoose, Nostalgia, Melancholia (a name I gave to my dead mother, who sometimes visits me at midnight, although her real name was Agnes).

In several of my student manifestations, as failed scholar-actor in college, I seemed quite good at minor but substantive roles be-cause I could eventually hear voices with great clarity, within my lines, once the actual words were settled upon the springboard of memory and my imagination, then I'd let fly. I enjoyed reading Polonius, that homily-headed doddering old fool. When I played Claudius, I employed Hugh High Hickles' voice to capture the conscience of the king.

My acting ability was quite limited—I see that now—because I could never move from hearing the voices to projecting a strong, singular interpretation. I got into arguments with directors in col-lege productions and a few community theatre companies about where the interpretation of the voice was taking me. I would argue fiercely for the integrity of playwright's voice and for his precise hearing of his characters' individual voices; but would they listen to my voice? Hell no!

Now as I reflect on these memories, I realize the directors heard the aspiring playwright playing havoc with their productions. They weren't dismissing me—indeed they were really listening to me—hearing that inner soul, so streaked by voices, and so alive to the vibrations of the voices within the character's lines. These directors were not tuning me out; yet I was not tuned in to where I wanted to go. I could pitch my apprentice instrument to the singularity of the voice with a surprising sensitivity given the limitations of my training and my talent—offstage. But I could never convey the voices really, that the individual playwright heard, babbling away in an individual character's soul. I was fitful and driven to take them on as I am tormented to take them over from within me. I understand this now. (I was always fascinated—even as a kid—by mimics, impersonators or impressionists. I remember seeing George Kirby scores of times—he was promoted as *the man with a thousand voices*.)

But why and how do these voices select me to do their talking and their bidding? To tell their troubles to? Why do they talk to me? Why do they come to me as some lost brother and work upon my consciousness? Upon two boards and a passion they project within the precincts of my soul. Why select me to fling them back out into orbit? Or back into our orbit? From which solar system did they re-emerge? Are they Flying Objects? I guess you might call Ford a Flying Objectionable.

Some of these departed souls surely can throw *me* into orbit, as they demand space within the precincts of my already weary, crowded consciousness. Certainly it seems they've unleashed boldly formed, bodily voices within me that I've rarely known in the light of day or in the dark of the silent night: wheezing ghosts that unleash my imagination to be ever-searching, open, collective, distilling, that make me yearn for stories and voices. Their returning and revolving presence spins me into *re*-creation as they transform themselves through me; and I, through their ever-expanding presence in my life, am *racked* forevermore.

In a different way, that fabulous liar, (Oscar) Williemain suffers under a similar fixation of hearing voices.

They are determined simply and cunningly to live. The bodily form in which these voices existed is long-gone or now decomposed food for worms. (Yorick's skull cannot talk; yet its remembered soul speaks to the Dane.) Othello reveals this of his handkerchief, "the worms were hallowed that did breed the silk, and it was dyed in mummy which the skillful conserved of maidens' hearts." Though it is filled with powers of nostalgia and warning for the Moor, his beloved Desdemona is as dumb to the voices from within the magic of its web, as an Eskimo might be to the chanting voices coded away for believers in a string of rosary beads blessed by a Pope of Renaissance Venice. Or take my friend Galloway Wheeler, the Shakespearean scholar, who can look into a glass of sour mash and hear the voice of the Bard, as he calls forth Hamlet's speech, "Oh what a peasant rogue and slave am I."

These souls, returned through voices, still maintain their spiritual essence, their old human meanness, their angularity, their roughhouse jagged-edged evolutionary claim and climb after the regenerative sources of the ladder up to life. Maintaining the drive to stay alive, they seek out those people who listen to them, who are hyper-aware, with antennae high and keen enough to hear their voices. They don't seek to *communicate*, that most abused of modern words they seek to live. They throw their voices out there, as electrical charges, with the fond hope, or prayer, that some son-ofabitch will pick up the vibrations, hook them up and run with their unharnessed spirits. For they are outlaw hitchhikers, with the spirit of hijackers, blessed with wings for stellar flight.

HENRY

LOUIS GATES, JR.

H

ENRY LOUIS GATES, JR., was born and raised in Mineral County, West Virginia. He graduated summa cum laude from Yale University with a degree in history, and was a London correspondent for *Time* magazine before receiving his Ph.D. in English literature from Cambridge University in England. He writes frequently for such publications as *Harper's, The New York Times Book Review, The New Yorker,* and the *Village Voice.* His books include *The Signifying Monkey* (1989), for which he received an American Book Award; *Reading Black, Reading Feminist* (1990); and *Loose Canons* (1992). His memoir, *Colored People* (1994), has met with tremendous success. He is the W.E.B. Du Bois Professor of Humanities and chairman of the Department of Afro-American Studies at Harvard University and is the coeditor of the award-winning *Transitions* magazine.

THE FIRST TIME I EVER considered myself a writer was when the accountant who was doing my income taxes wrote down *writer* as my occupation—he had to put that in order to make deductions. I remember wanting to erase it because it felt too grand. It's one thing to write book reviews, quite another to be Henry James.

My father told stories all the time when I was growing up. My mother used to call them "lies." I didn't know that "lies" was the name for stories in the black vernacular, I just thought it was her own word that she had made up. I was inspired by those "lies," though, and knew that I wanted to tell some too one day.

When I was ten or twelve, I had a baseball column in the local newspaper. I was the scorekeeper for the minor-league games in my town—I would compile all of the facts, and then the editor and I would put together a narrative. I did that every week during the summer. The best part was seeing my name in print. After that, I was hooked—hooked to seeing my name in black and white on paper.

At fourteen or fifteen, I read James Baldwin's work and became fascinated with the idea of writing. When I started reading about black people through the writings of black people, suddenly I was seized by the desire to write. I was in awe of how writers were able to take words and create an illusion of the world that people could step into—a world where people opened doors and shut doors, fell in love and out of love, where people lived and died. I wanted to be able to create those worlds too. I knew I had a voice even before I knew what a "writer's voice" meant. I didn't know what it was, but I could hear it, and I knew when my rhythm was on—it was almost as if I could hear myself write. I thought I had a unique take on the world and trusted my sensibility. It struck me that perhaps it would be a good thing to share it with other people.

I used to keep a commonplace book where I would write down quotes—a book that I read was either good or bad depending upon how many quotes I got out of it. Basically, I copied down James Baldwin's whole books! I discovered Baldwin during the civil rights movement, a time when I was wrestling with my own identity as a black person, and a time when I was also obsessed with this white woman in my class who didn't like me because I was black. That situation really messed with me. Baldwin's anger, clarity, and insight into the black experience was tremendously helpful and timely for me.

When I was little, I really wanted to be a painter. My mother could draw very well, and I remember thinking how magical it was that she could create these images on paper. It didn't flash through my mind until much later that writing might also be a way to create imagery. I devoured books, but everybody in my family read a lot. My father liked to read mystery and detective novels, and *Alfred Hitchcock's Mystery Magazine* came every month. We always had all sorts of magazines around the house. I was very good at English in school, seemed to have a talent with words, and went to the library often, but I didn't think much of it. I used to admire storytellers but was afraid to speak in front of people. I was absolutely petrified at the thought of standing up in public with a whole lot of people looking.

I knew as a child that there would be a calling for me, but in many ways it is hard for me now to believe what I have become, and the influence that I have on other people as an educator, a writer, and as a race leader—I mean, I grew up in a village. But in some capacity, even as a very young boy, I know that I envisioned being part of this world that I am now a part of. I knew that instinctively, and I can attribute Baldwin's work as one of the passageways to this world. More than that, though, I wanted to be in a world where I could write about love and death. I wanted to write novels.

I went to Yale to be a doctor, a career I was slated for long before I had a say in the matter, so it became a constant struggle for me to repress my urge to write. The same thought would come back to me over and over: what you really want to be is a writer. I would have to push that thought back down. In my sophomore year of college, my girlfriend and I were sitting on my bed one Saturday night, and I said in passing, "Well, when I'm a doctor . . ." She said, "That's the biggest bunch of bullshit—look at the books on your shelf. They are all about literature, history, or black studies—there isn't one book up there about medicine." The next day I ran to the bookstore and bought a book on medicine.

I spent my junior year of college in Tanzania, where I worked in a mission hospital giving general anesthesia, which was boring as hell. It was infinitely interesting being with people, but I knew that I didn't want to cut people open. I found it very mechanical. I wanted to *write* about people who cut people open. Upon my return from Africa, some friends of mine, who were editors at the *Yale Daily News*, asked me to write a column for the paper. I started writing about my experiences in Africa and about being black. I got a very wide and positive reception for the columns and knew that I was on to something. After I graduated from Yale, I went to Cambridge University in England. I was simultaneously offered a job at the London bureau of *Time* magazine, so half of the time I was at Cambridge, and half of the time I was at *Time*. *Time* ended up offering me a permanent job, on the condition that I would have to move every three years, which seemed to me a fate worse than death. Furthermore, I wasn't at all committed to the idea of being a journalist. It was fiction writing that I was drawn to.

The life of a writer was so unsure, and such a risk, that I couldn't quite give into it. I didn't want to be living hand to mouth—it would have been too terrible. I did not want to be poor. I wanted stability, and if I was going to write, I wanted to write when I wanted to write and what I wanted to write—like I can now. But it was hard to get here; you either have to chase fire trucks and work your way up in an organization, or you have to establish another career as a professor and a literary critic. I established myself as a professor. With that decision came a very public role that evolved rather slowly.

I didn't know anything about black literature, or really any literature, nor did I start studying it as a literary critic until I went to study at Cambridge, where I met Nobel Prize laureate Wole Soyinka, who was my supervisor. I learned that there are all kinds of subcategories of literature—American literature, English literature, women's literature, African-American literature. These are all part of a larger class called "literature." Black literature is not qualitatively different from other national literatures. It is one major branch of literature and is its own tradition, but how could it be fundamentally different from other literatures?

Most black writers learn to write by reading other white writers, and most black texts are mulatto—they have complex ancestors, they are two-toned. My generation, and certainly the generation of college students today, read a lot of black authors and situate ourselves, but some black authors will claim that they have never read or studied other black authors. The way that I perceive black literature, and have taught it in the past and present, is similar to links in a chain among texts: *The Invisible Man* rewrites *Native Son*, *Native Son* rewrites *Their Eyes Were*

Watching God, *Their Eyes Were Watching God* rewrites *Cane*— all of these narratives echo and riff on each other, like jazz compositions, or improvisations.

In England, being an academic was certainly the highest calling, and being a lawyer or a doctor was what people who couldn't be academics did. It was a different hierarchal universe for me. Soyinka and I started reading together, which I found very exciting. Soyinka was sublime. He taught me about drinking wine, smoking cigars, and writing well. I began to think about myself more and more as an intellectual and was falling ever more deeply in love with words. I came back from Cambridge and went to Yale Law School for thirty days. After I dropped out of law school, I was hired as a secretary in the Department of Afro-American Studies at Yale, which service I rendered from October 1, 1975, to June 30, 1976, at midnight, at which time I became a lecturer in English and Afro-American Studies. Shortly thereafter, Toni Morrison got me my first assignment with the *New York Times Book Review*. She told me to call the editor there, and to use her name. I did, and it worked. After that, I began to write reviews for *The Times Literary Supplement*, *The Spectator*, and various other publications.

I don't think that the prime reason for writing is to save the world, or to save black people. I do it because it makes me feel good. I want to record my vision and to entertain people. When I was writing reviews, although it was an intriguing way to discuss literature, I would have a lot of black people say to me, "I'm having a hard time understanding you, brother." I've always had two conflicting voices within me, one that wants to be outrageous and on the edge, always breaking new ground, and another that wants to be loved by the community for that outrageousness. It is very difficult to expect that people will let you have it both ways like that. Those who really care about a community are the ones who push the boundaries and create new definitions, but generally they get killed for doing that, which is what I mean when I refer to myself as a griot in the black community—the one who makes the wake-up call, who loves his people enough to truly examine the status quo.

The wonderful thing about *Colored People* is that everybody gets it and can appreciate it because it is a universal story. It is my segue from nonfiction to fiction. I wrote it to preserve a world that has passed away, and to reveal some secrets—not for the shock value, but because I want to re-create a voice that black people use when there are no white people around. Oftentimes in black literature, black authors get all lockjawed in their writing because they are doing it for a white audience, and not for themselves. You don't hear the voice of black people when it's just us in the kitchen, talking out the door and down the road, and that is the voice that I am trying to capture in *Colored People*. Integration may have cost us that voice. We cannot take it for granted and must preserve it whenever possible. I don't know what kind of positive language and linguistic rituals are being passed down in the fragmented, dispossessed black underclass. I think it's very different from when and where I was raised, when there was a stronger sense of community, and that language was everywhere I turned.

The poignancy of the gap between my memories of growing up and the reality that surrounds me every time I go back to Piedmont (my hometown) tears me up. My mother is dead, and my father is eighty. I used to think that I would always go back to Piedmont, but after my father dies, I can't imagine any reason why I ever would. A lot of my remaining family is gonna go crazy when they read this book. The secret story of my family is that my grandmother had two lovers, and when she got pregnant, she picked the wrong man as the father, because when the baby was born, he looked just like the other lover. Nobody has ever talked about that secret, and it has never been revealed until now. That baby was my uncle Jim—alias Nemo—and I told his son, Little Jim, about the secret because I needed to get him ready. But I didn't tell anyone else that I was writing about it. In that way, the book is definitely a memoir.

I love anecdotes, and in my writing up until *Colored People*, mostly critical essays, I would usually start with an anecdote of some sort. There would always be autobiographical references. I had been sneaking up on the memoir for a long time, and after my first year as the chair of Afro-American Studies at Harvard, I went to Bellagio to write it. When I arrived at the airport in Bellagio, I had been at a conference in Italy and was exhausted. It was a very rainy night, and the roads to my hotel were very narrow and curvy. I got so sick I thought I would vomit. I went to bed green, and when I woke up the next morning, I literally threw open the shutters in my room and saw the most beautiful landscape I had ever seen. My view looked out over a lake, and suddenly it reminded me of my hometown, Piedmont, and the way that it looked out over a river. I got a quick cup of coffee, and then sat down and wrote twenty pages.

I wrote about how my daughter Maggie had at one point found my mother unattractive. Maggie told me this after my mother died, and at the time, I couldn't believe that Maggie would say such a thing. And then I remembered how I had always found my father's mother unattractive. An editor had suggested that I write the memoir in the form of letters to my daughters, Maggie and Liza, which is the way that *Colored People* was first drafted. But that didn't work because there is so much sex in the book. I changed the format but didn't stop thinking about my daughters because it was inspirational to feel that I was passing something on to them. I ended up writing twenty pages a day for two weeks while I was in Bellagio. Often I didn't know where the writing was going to go, but I believed in it, and let it come. The authorization of telling the story came in the form of pen and paper—it was time to tell the story, and the story came.

Everybody can look at the same phenomenon, but to be able to analyze it and to make people see it in a different light is exciting. There is nothing more gratifying to me than when a reader writes back, "Dr. Gates, I never thought of it that way."

From
COLORED PEOPLE

For many of the colored people in Piedmont—and for a lot of the older Colemans in particular—integration was experienced as a loss. The warmth and nurturance of the womblike colored world was slowly and inevitably disappearing, in a process that really began on the day they closed the door for the last time at Howard School, back in 1956. Within our family, integration anxiety played itself out broadly in terms of generations; those who had graduated from the colored high school found the adjustment much harder than those who had gone only to the segregated elementary school, if that. A principal focus of the resulting tension was the raising of children—the issues of their rights and responsibilities and their relation to authority, both white and familial. I heard it times beyond counting: That boy's got too much mouth. And from their perspective, my brother and I probably did have too much mouth. Faced with what must have been a painful choice between her loyalty to her brothers and her loyalty to the sons whose independence she nurtured and encouraged, my mother never wavered. Much to the chagrin of the Coleman clan, she always took our side.

Clearly, the way she raised her children was perceived by them as a threat: it represented chaos, disrespect for tradition, order, containment. And it was reckless—insufficiently heedful of the fact that the white world could crush us all anytime it wanted to. Because I flouted the rules, they thought I would come to a bad end, and they took pleasure in letting me know that. Deep down, I think they were frightened for me. And deeper down, I think I frightened them.

Raymond could scarcely bear to set eyes on me. When are you going to get that nappy shit cut? he'd ask me, looking balefully at my still tentative Afro. Boy, sometimes I wonder about you. He and his brothers called me alternately "Malcolm" and "Stokely," and did so with the purest derision.

The way I figured, they just didn't get it. Maybe most of the colored people in Piedmont still didn't. But my friends did. We were a black consciousness cultural club. We began to read books together, black books, and to discuss them—Claude Brown, Eldridge Cleaver, Ralph Ellison, and Malcolm X. I could order them through Red Bowls, pay for them with the money I got redeeming bottles.

Back in eighth grade, I had seen W.E.B. Du Bois's photograph in our history textbook, stuck near the end of the section on the twentieth century, like a black-and-white postage stamp. (We never got to the civil rights chapters in our textbooks.) "He's a Communist," was Daddy's contribution to black history. I couldn't wait to read him, though it wouldn't be till college.

Now, two years later, I did a book report for Mrs. Iverson on Dick Gregory's new autobiography, *Nigger*, and a battle of wills ensued: about her saying the title. She refused. I had said it first, but her awkwardness made the word sound dirty, even in my mouth. Most of all, I remember the funny shade of crimson Mrs. Iverson's face took on when the nurtured crescendo of my oral presentation somehow culminated on that word: "*nigger.*" And I sat down to silence, part of me satisfied, part of me frightened, but all the time knowing I had passed through some kind of gate. Unlike the bottles I sold to Red, I was nonreturnable.

We'd just gone through the summer of 1966, the summer when Stokely Carmichael announced something he called "Black Power" and many of the Negroes became black people and grew big Afros and started wearing dashikis and beads. I got goose bumps just thinking about being *black*, being proud of being black and learning to look at bushed-up kinky hair and finding it beautiful. KKK hair, Daddy called it: Knotty, Kinky, and Kan't-comby.

To older generations, we must have looked like freaks in a carnival, walking around muttering the few Swahili phrases we had managed to memorize, giving each other complicated soul handshakes, and putting our clenched fists over our hearts and saying things like "my beautiful black brothers and sisters." And in some ways it seems funny to me now. But it was an exciting and sincere effort to forge a new communal identity among a people descended from splendid ancient cultures, abducted and forced into servility, and now deprived of collective economic and political power. We thought we had learned at last our unutterable, secret name, and that name was BLACK. We believed that if we uttered it again and again, like an incantation, we would move mountains just as surely as Ali Baba had done, or knock down barriers like Joshua, who fit the battle of Jericho and the walls came tumbling down.

This people who had spent a couple of hundred years ironing, frying, greasing, and burning their hair, doing everything but pulling it out by its roots in an attempt to make it unkinky, had all of a sudden become converts to a new religion, the Holy Order of the Natural Kink. It drew sharp divisions in our communities: B.C. and A.D.—Before Crinkle and After Da Straightener. An Afro looked like a crown of cultural glory on the right head. If you took care of your Afro, kept the split ends cut, and washed and combed it regularly, it could emerge like a radiant halo of blackness. Cotton candy of kinkiness. Bad hair was now "good," and lots of people with "good" hair—especially the guiltily light-complected—were busy trying to kink theirs up. The world had turned upside down. Light-complected people were attempting to become darker, to distance and deny their white ancestors, intruders in their genetic line. One-fifth Yoruba, one-fifth Ashanti, one-fifth Mandinka, one-fifth this, and one-fifth that . . .

Of course, our consciousness was still at a relatively early stage, with respect to the emerging creed of blackness, and there were other things to preoccupy the Fearsome Foursome. Most of all we had my daddy. My three friends had no relationships with their fathers. Roy was too busy drinking and carousing, Swano never did have a daddy, and Fisher's father, Mr. Ben, seemed aloof and distant. Roland and I were born in the same hospital, three days apart, and his father always said that he picked up the wrong baby. I would have been crushed under that burden.

So by the time I was sixteen, my buddies had adopted my daddy as their surrogate father, and the four of us would sit for hours arguing with Daddy and Mama, eating dinner, watching television, and arguing some more. Vietnam, Black Power, Dr. King, Stokely, Afros, the Panthers, the time of day. We'd fall asleep in my bedroom, the four of us, then get up and argue with the Old Man some more. We'd argue with Daddy for hours on end. You boys are *crazy*, he'd say when he wanted a break. You're as crazy as Skip. We'd watch the riots, watch the convention, watch the bombings, watch the entire news. We were close enough to D.C. that I could buy the *Washington Post* every day, so I read it during lunch at school and would share the results with the fellas.

We watched the war together, we watched the King assassination together, we watched Bobby Kennedy's assassination together. Daddy always had been a conspiracy buff; he hated Lynchin' Johnson, as he called him, and was convinced in November of 1963 that *he* had killed JFK.

The irony was, Daddy wasn't much more in sympathy with my new politics and hairstyle than the Colemans; yet the things that would divide me from the Colemans provided a point of contact for Daddy and me. For one thing, after years of ritual silence, even argument was an improvement. And arguing—a playful give-and-take—would prove the means by which we rebuilt our relationship, establishing a camaraderie broad enough to include my friends, as well.

For us, the Fearsome Foursome, part of discovering politics was trying to be political ourselves. The Fearsome organized the first school boycott in the history of Piedmont. All the black kids stayed home on the day of the King funeral—and got bad citizenship grades in return. Some of us attended prayer vigils, like the one we organized at the Episcopal church.

Not until my late teens did I learn that we weren't quite the pioneers of protest we imagined ourselves to be. It turned out that what was now the Holiness church was once the colored elementary school. Some years before I was born, Mama and practically the whole colored town led a civil rights march demanding the right of the colored to be educated, if only in their own schools. The way it had been, you went only to the eighth grade in the one-room school, then had to ride the bus to Cumberland to attend George Washington Carver School, which is where Daddy met Mama. But that the Coleman family, aside from Mama, was much involved in that protest was something I greatly doubted.

If Mama's tolerance separated her from her brethren, Daddy's intolerance, jocular though it was, separated him from his. Indeed, the other Gateses were positively approving toward me and my budding political ideas. You couldn't style an Afro with hair as good as theirs, but they were freethinkers and, as such, welcomed me into their ranks.

CHARLES JOHNSON

CHARLES JOHNSON was born in Illinois in 1948. He received his B.A. in journalism and his M.A. in philosophy from Southern Illinois University. Johnson has written three novels: *Faith and the Good Thing* (1974); *Oxherding Tale* (1982), which won the Washington State Governor's Award for Literature in 1983; and *Middle Passage* (1990), which won the National Book Award in 1990. His numerous stories, essays, and reviews have appeared in such publications as *Antaeus, Mother Jones, The New York Times Book Review,* the *Los Angeles Times,* and *American Book Review*. He has been the recipient of the Callaloo Creative Writing Award and the Journalism Alumnus of the Year Award at Southern Illinois University. He is currently professor of English at the University of Washington and lives in Seattle with his wife and two children.

CALL MYSELF AN ARTIST. I don't call myself a *writer*—that was never a goal. The goal was simply to create.

When I was a kid, nothing was more delightful to me than drawing. In elementary school, that is what I got a pat on the head for. All I wanted to do with my life was to draw. Nothing was more interesting to me than the fact that creating art began as an internal and private thought or feeling that no one could see, which then became externalized on a piece of paper where everyone could see! I wanted to fill the world with images. So I thought of myself as an artist. I wrote in high school and published stories in the school paper, but writing was really just a sideline for me.

What I discovered early on is that one art form will inevitably lead you to another. My interest in literature was always present, but I was more focused on drawing. I read a lot, maybe one or two books a week, whatever I could get my hands on. And then when I got to college, I became fascinated with philosophy. I was a journalism major because it provided a way for me to publish my drawings, political satire; but suddenly philosophy spoke to me more deeply than any other discipline.

It became very important for me to write when I realized the limitations of other mediums. There are certain things that I can and cannot do with caricature as a cartoonist. I began to understand that there were things that I could only achieve through written language, and so it was necessary for me to move on to various literary forms. Then I learned that there were things I could do with nonfiction writing that I couldn't do with novel writing, and that there were things I can do with novel writing that I couldn't do with short stories, and so on. Each genre of writing allowed me to explore my subjects using the means of each unique and specific medium.

After I graduated from college and had been working as a journalist for a while, I knew that I wanted to find a longer form of writing. Journalism gave me the opportunity to do features, but that was about as artistic as it got. I was attracted to a longer form of writing basically because I had an idea in my mind that would not leave me alone. I had the character and the situation for a novel, and during the course of any given day, more frequently as I was about to go to bed, I would get another image or another idea based around this character and this situation. The only way to deal with this idea was to write it into existence. I don't feel as though the novel was really any good by the time I completed it, but I had accomplished something that I had never accomplished before, which was 250 pages of fiction.

Knowing that I could always write 250 pages, I decided to write another novel, but this time I wanted to try to improve on character development, plot, and structure. I kept writing and writing, and ended up writing six novels in two years. By the time I started writing the seventh novel, I had read every handbook on the craft of writing that I could find and still wasn't exactly sure of what I was doing. I realized that what I needed was a good teacher. I needed somebody who had more experience than I did and who could address the issues that I was not able to find in the handbooks, such as matters of voice and prose rhythm. I signed up for a class with John Gardner, who at the time had just published and received critical acclaim for his book *Grendel*.

Imagination cannot be taught. You cannot teach someone a sense of how to write, nor can you teach how to adapt to the long-term dedication and drive of a prose writer. I never thought that writing could be taught, but I do think that guidance is tremendously helpful, since writing is such an isolated craft. It has been estimated by some literary critics that it takes fiction writers fifteen years to become established as writers, beginnning after they have been published for the first time. I find that to be fairly true with most of the writers I know. Eighty percent of first-time novelists do not publish a second novel. John Gardner went for fifteen years as a very underpublished writer, with brilliant fiction spilling out of his closet. When he finally wrote a best-seller, he brought a book out every six months—books that were already written.

When I met Gardner, I was more or less a literary innocent. I think he actually appreciated that. I didn't come with any presuppositions, all I wanted to do was to tell stories. I really had no interest in what the "writer's life" was. I was a philosophy major. It was ironic because in my experience, philosophy majors always had this sort of contemptuous attitude toward English majors, accusing them of not thinking clearly! Gardner introduced me to his friends and other writers he knew across the country because of his recent fame at that time. I didn't then, and I still don't now, have what anyone would call "literary ambition." I guess I don't really know what that means. What I do know is that I have always loved great stories—I love to read them, and I *love* to write them.

Gardner was a very unusual man. My experience with him as my mentor was interesting because we had a lot in common. We both believed that moral issues pertained to literature. I had specific questions as a philosophy student—I was getting my master's degree in philosophy at the time—about philosophical fiction and how one went about writing it. John Gardner was a philosophical writer. I had always felt that there was a void in black literature that could be filled in the area of the black philosophical novel. We discussed three writers who I felt were philosophical novelists: Jean Toomer and his novel *Cane*, because of its very Eastern orientation, and his association with Gurdjieff, and also his novel fits very well within the American transcendental tradition going back to Emerson and Thoreau; Richard Wright, who was very orientated toward Marxism and certainly existentialism, even before he went to Paris and met Sartre; and then of course Ralph Ellison and his novel *Invisible Man*, which is very much a Freudian adventure but is also about the nature of perception. We have two thousand years of Western philosophy, and even more of Eastern philosophy. I figured that black writers could contribute something to this. The question was: how to do it?

Gardner was very helpful in terms of figuring out a way to pursue black philosophical writing not so much directly in the things he said, but rather indirectly by allowing me to watch him approach his own fiction. Once he realized that I could write, he made it clear that I should hold in contempt any sentence I wrote that fell below the level of the best writing that I had ever written. He strongly emphasized that I should write with fairness for all of my characters. Gardner was very serious about morality in fiction; you do not set characters up as one dimensional, you do not abuse characters for your own purposes whether they are religious or political or for any other reason—every character must be given his or her own moment of realization on the page, whether we as writers like them or not.

There were times when I abused characters in my writing, and Gardner would write in the margins, "Shame on you!" I would have to go back and think about why I was setting up a character to be disliked. Eventually I understood that it was far better to explore how a human being could arrive at the situation he or she was in rather than sabotage the character because I thought he or she was unlikeable. Fiction writing was for Gardner what it very soon became for me—a mode of knowledge; a mode of understanding others, and by virtue of that understanding, understanding oneself.

It is a loaded question to ask what the differences may or may not be between black philosophy and white philosophy. When we speak of philosophers, by the very nature of the discipline, we are almost immediately speaking about individual figures. We don't talk about "white" philosophy, we talk about the philosophy of Descartes or of Bacon. There is no monolithic thing called "white" philosophy, nor is there such a thing called Eastern philosophy; there is Taoism—but the individual thinkers within that philosophy cannot be lumped together. I'm not sure what black philosophy is. I think the best material written on this subject is by Kwame Anthony Appiah in his book *In My Father's House.* Appiah understands what the philosophical enterprise is, which is mainly the effort to raise interesting questions, and to try and grapple with the meaning of the world and of the universe in an intelligible way. And although he is black, his theories can be applied cross-racially and cross-culturally.

Trying to figure out what makes a philosophy black is like trying to figure out what makes a person black. The very concept implies that there is a black essence, or a black nature. If there is a black essence, then that deprives us all of our free will. If there is an essence that we call blackness, an essence that actually pertains to a philosophy or a person, then the capability of changing from that essence is not possible. Look at it this way—we've got nouns and we've got verbs, we've got product and we've got process; something that is a product and a noun like say, blackness, is dead, it has no capacity for change, evolution, and growth. Essentialistic thought is damaging not just to black people, but to all people. Existence precedes essence.

I love the fact that writing is a process of discovery. I can have a few ideas in my mind that I want to work out through writing, and by the time I am finished, I have discovered so much more. Ninety percent of writing is rewriting. Writing is not about sitting down to write what you already think. As I think August Wilson once put it to me: "You write to figure out *what* you think." That is exciting, and every project, no matter whether it is a book review or an extended essay, offers that promise of self-revelation and some kind of revelation about the world.

Any fiction or story reveals the writer's life. Any pimples, warts, whatever in the story are in him—the writer cannot hide behind his fiction. Every character will reveal the writer because the novel is a product of the writer's mind, spirit, and emotions. By the same token, in my writing I almost never use autobiographical incidents from my life. Sometimes I will see a human-interest article in the newspaper, or a friend may tell me a story about himself that is anecdotal, and that may work its way into my writing. Some of my short stories and the novel *Oxherding Tale* take place in the antebellum South, so I had to imagine various incidents in that setting. All of the raw material that the imagination uses comes in one way or another from the world. There is an intimate correlation between world and writing, but not necessarily in terms of the literal biography of the writer and the writing. Writers take material from the world in order to reinvent a fictive universe.

Middle Passage took place on a slave ship in 1830, so the literal events of my life could not possibly have been placed in that novel. Nevertheless, I may hear a line of dialogue in conversation with a friend or a family member that I may then use in my writing. For example, when I was maybe eight or nine years old, I remember my mother once introduced me to one of her friends. This older woman looked down at me as we met and said, "You know, the reason I look so bad is because I been livin'." I never forgot that. In an entirely different set of circumstances, one of the characters says that very line of dialogue to another character in *Middle Passage*. The statement gives the sense that somebody may look a little more than tired if they have been living life to its maximum potential.

On the other hand, I wrote a story called "Exchange Value" about two boys who break into a miser's house with the intention of robbery but who discover much more than they had antici- pated. I read the story once in Paris, and during the Q & A session afterward someone asked me if I had ever broken into somebody's house. The question really threw me. I didn't understand why any- one would even ask me that.

The very best-case scenario in terms of the writer's life appear- ing in his writing by way of emotional autobiography is when the evolution of a writer's thoughts and feelings are present in the text. When this happens, the reader can get a sense of the writer's per- ceptions, values, and interpretations. It is like reading an autobiog- raphy of the soul.

The hardest part about writing for me is getting myself out of the way. If I have a good story and can see the inherent potential in it, the hard part is removing myself and being a good midwife while assisting the story's birth. Whatever personal problems and prejudices I may be having while the story is being born need to be put aside. Because the story and its people need a lot of room to develop and to go in the direction that their *natures* require them to go in. The story needs to be able to arrive at its own implicit and inherent logical resolution, as opposed to arriving at where I would like it to arrive.

In the beginning stages of writing a story, I do a lot of knock- ing at the door. If I do enough that's right, then the door springs open and the story lives. This is usually after trying a whole bunch of wrong approaches that I thought were right, and I feel a tremendous amount of fatigue. But once the story begins to breathe on its own, it doesn't even feel like I am writing anymore. It is like I am watching the events of the story unfold in my imagination, and I am just trying to keep up with it. It's almost like dreaming.

I like to think that my writing may be something beautiful and/or something helpful to another person. Ultimately, the writer is a servant. I think that every work we do should be done in the spirit of giving, not for any exterior motives. Not for money, not for attention. Writing is a gift. I can think of many pieces of writing I have read over the years that have been precisely that for me. I read a poem once about the blessing of life. Clichéd as it may sound, the poet was able to communicate that blessing in a way that I was able to feel in my depths. I will be forever grateful to that poet.

I've never thought of writing as a job or as a career. It's not like being a stockbroker. I write because I have no choice, and if I don't do it I don't feel right. It's like having a big piece of stone that I keep chipping away at to get rid of everything that isn't the face. And what keeps me chipping away is the promise of what I know that face can look like.

━━━

From
MIDDLE PASSAGE
Entry, the third
June 23, 1830

Forty-one days after leaving New Orleans, we coasted in on calm waters, a breeze at our backs, and the skipper set all hands to unmooring the ship, bringing her slowly like a hearse to anchorage alongside the trading post at Bangalang. It was a rowdy fort, all right. Cringle told me the barracoons were built by the Royal African Company in 1683—one of several well-fortified western forts always endangered by hostile, headhunting natives nearby, by competing merchants, and over two centuries residents at the fort had fought first the Dutch, then the French for control of Negro slaves. Lately, it had fallen into the soft, uncallused hands of Owen Bogha, the halfbreed son of a brutal slave trader from Liverpool and the black princess of a small tribe on the Rio Pongo. He was a sensualist. A powdered fop and Anglophile who dyed his chest and pubic hairs blond and, as did other men of the day plagued by head lice big as beans, shaved his pate and wore perfumed wigs. Educated in England, this man Bogha, who greatly enjoyed wealth and the same gaming tables played by Captain Falcon in Paris, returned to take advantage of his father's property and mother's prestige in Bangalang, overseeing from his great hilltop home the many warehouses, bazaars, harems, and Moslem caravans that crawled from the interior during the Dry Season. The skipper stayed at his home most nights, consuming stuffed fish and raisin wine, and giving Bogha news of "civilization" back in England and America—he was starving for news, claimed Bogha, in this filthy, Godforsaken hole. And Cringle, being an officer, was invited too, but said he couldn't abide flesh merchants; in fact, he abhorred everything about Bangalang, and slept instead with the rest of the crew on deck in the open air to escape the heat below.

As for myself, I was simply glad to be ashore. It had been unsettling and claustrophobic, out there with the ship cleaving waves the color of root medicine, soughing wind that broke the spider-web tracery of rigging like thread, and the sky and sea blurred together into a pewter gray gloom without a stitch, without outlines, without a bottom to their depths, and sometimes, when we could not see the horizon and sailed through endless fog and shifting mist, I'd felt such dizzying entrapment—of being deprived of such basic directions as left and right, up and down—that I screamed myself awake some nights, choking on the rank male sweat that hung around my hammock like wet clothing. I ached from cleaning pots in the cookroom, and I'd grown tired of my clothes being so perpetually wet from deckwash, the slap of rainwind, and leaks in the orlop that once I had the feeling that the toes on my left foot were webbed. On top of that, Cringle had shouted at me so often for being slow, or asleep during my watch, that I could tell you which of his teeth had been worked on in Boston or Philadelphia, pulled in another city or by a dentist in New Orleans. I wished in vain for dry breeches, floorboards that didn't move, a bowl of warm milk at bedtime, and sometimes—aye—for Isadora. Worse, I kept a light cold, and my incessant coughing gave me headaches. Even so, I could not join the others in their banter after we lowered anchor, or even drink with much gusto—stale beer gave me the johnny-trots—but simply lie quietly in my bunk, wondering if in a single fantastic evening I had become Captain Ebenezer Falcon's shipboard bride.

I could express this fear to no one, and I beg you to keep it to yourself. His courtship of me, for so it must be called, began the night Falcon caught me rummaging through his cabin. This was not an easy situation to explain away. Especially after what I learned from his papers, ledgers, and journal. Somehow I'd miscalculated. According to his schedule, the skipper should have been at the fort all evening, unloading four skiffs freighted with clothing and beads, liquor, and utensils of brass and pewter for the notorious Arab trader Ahman-de-Bellah, whose first caravan of captured Negroes from eight, maybe nine tribes, was herded into Bangalang a few hours before. Falcon's curtains were drawn. His door was padlocked. Of course that presented no problem for me.

Slipping away from my watch and into his room, easing his door shut with my fingertips, I felt the change come over me, a familiar, sensual tingle that came whenever I broke into someone's home, as if I were slipping inside another's soul. Everything must be done slowly, deliberately, first the breath coming deep from the belly, easily, as if the room itself were breathing, limbs light like hollow reeds, free of tension, all parts of me flowing as a single piece, for I had learned in Louisiana that in balletlike movements there could be no error of the body, no elbows cracking into chair arms in a stranger's space to give me away. Theft, if the truth be told, was the closest thing I knew to transcendence. Even better, it broke the power of the propertied class, which pleased me. As a boy I'd never had enough of anything. Yes, my brother Jackson and I lived close to our master, but on the Makanda farm during the leaner years, life was, as old bondwomen put it, "too little too late." At suppertime: watery soup and the worst part of the hog and so little of that that Jackson often skipped meals secretly so I could have a little bit more. If you have never been hungry, you cannot know the *either/or* agony created by a single sorghum biscuit—either your brother gets it or you do. And if you *do* eat it, you know in your bones you have stolen the food straight from his mouth, there being so little for either of you. This was the daily, debilitating side of poverty that no one speaks of, the perpetual scarcity that, at every turn, makes the simplest act a moral dilemma. On a nearby farm there lived a slave father and his two sons who had one blouse and pair of breeches among them, so that when one went off to work the others were left naked and had to hide at home in their shed. True enough, Jackson and I fared better than they, but in linen handed down by Reverend Chandler or by his pious friends—who no doubt felt good about the very charity that annihilated me—in their scented waistcoats and smelly boots I whiffed the odor of other men, even heard their accents echo in the very English I spoke, as if I was no one—or nothing—in my own right, and I wondered how in God's name you could *have* anything if circumstances threw you amongst the *had*. Ah, me. The Reverend's prophecy that I would grow up to be a picklock was wiser than he knew, for was I not, as a Negro in the New World, *born* to be a thief? Or, put less harshly, inheritor of two millennia of things I had not myself made? But enough of this.

On ship I decided against my usual signatures of defiance: pooping amiddlemost a local politician's satin pillow, for example, or fabricating for his wife—some blue-blooded snob—a love letter from their black chambermaid that was worthy of James Cleveland, or simply scrawling on their parlor wall in charcoal from their hearth, as I often did, "I can enter your life whenever I wish." No, I did none of this, there in Falcon's quarters. All I wanted was to know his heart (if he had one) and to walk off, as was reasonable, with a tradable trinket or two.

I drifted from object to object at first, just touching things with sweat-tipped fingers as a way to taint and take hold of them—to loose them from their owner—but ever more slowly, for I soon found that Falcon's room was ingeniously rigged with exploding, trip-lever booby traps. He'd filled ordinary rum bottles on his shelf with liquid explosives (each detonated by a pull-friction fuse in the cork), and two of his calabash pipes had stems packed with gunpowder. Also he kept all the ship's weapons in his cabin under lock and key. These security measures (or perhaps they spoke of Falcon's insecurity) I expected, but not what I found next. His biggest crates of plunder from every culture conceivable, which he covered with tarp at the rear of the room, were wrenched open, spilling onto the sloping floor bird-shaped Etruscan vases, Persian silk prayer carpets, and portfolios of Japanese paintings on rice paper. Temple scrolls I found, precious tablets, and works so exotic to my eyes that Falcon's crew of fortune hunters could have taken them only by midnight raids and murder. Slowly, it came to me, like the sound of a stone plunked into a pond, that he had a standing order from his financiers, powerful families in New Orleans who underwrote the *Republic*, to stock Yankee museums and their homes with whatever of value was not nailed down in the nations he visited. To bring back slaves, yes, but to salvage the best of their war-shocked cultures too.

YUSEF

KOMUNYAKAA

Y

USEF KOMUNYAKAA won the Pulitzer Prize for Poetry in 1994 for his collection *Neon Vernacular: New and Selected Poems*. The book had previously won the Kingsley-Tufts Poetry Award from the Claremont Graduate School in Claremont, California. Other books of poetry by Komunyakaa include *Magic City* (1992), which vividly evokes the poet's childhood in Bogalusa, Louisiana; *Dien Cai Dau* (1988), which deals with his experience in the Vietnam War; *I Apologize for the Eyes in My Head* (1986), winner of the San Francisco Poetry Award; and *Copacetic* (1984). He is professor of English at Indiana University and was recently the Holloway Lecturer at the University of California, Berkeley.

POETRY IS THE PRIMARY MEDIUM I have chosen because of the conciseness, the precision, the imagery, and the music in the lines. I think of language as our first music.

I wrote one long poem in high school that was about a hundred lines long, very traditional with rhyme and quatrains. I continued to read poetry and whatever literature I could get at the time. I had very limited access to poetry and literature in Bogalusa, Louisiana, where I grew up. I read the traditional works of such writers as Shakespeare and Edgar Allen Poe. Only recently have I realized that I was introduced to African-American literature in what was termed "the Negro history way," which was the brief section in high school when we would study the history of African-American people. That is when I came in contact with Langston Hughes, Paul Lawrence Dunbar, and Phyllis Wheatly. It was a very short part of my education before we were back to the regular curriculum, and I was back to reading the history and literature dominated by Europeans.

In the works of Langston Hughes, I remember being struck by the surprise of his poetry and that it was so close to a spoken diction, with a kind of blues, metric shape. It was so immediate, and it touched my existence in a complete way. The poetry of Phyllis Wheatly was something I could meditate on. She wasn't as forthright and clear as Hughes, but there was a thread of language in her poems that was inviting.

I grew up in a poor and impoverished neighborhood in the deep South, dominated by the typical American, Calvinistic work ethic for the most part. People around me believed that if they worked hard enough they could get ahead in the "American

Dream," which of course was a complete myth. When I was growing up, I did not see it as a myth, but having been away from that part of my life for so long now, and in trying to establish some kind of intellectual equation, the "American Dream" seems to have been very much a myth.

There were six children in my family, and there was always a kind of interest, and a kind of energy, in activity surrounding me. Many times I would read poetry in order to establish a moment of contemplation, and other times I would go sight-seeing in the wooded areas around my house to allow myself moments of solitude. Those two escapes came together for me in ways that I am only able to understand now with some distance. I don't know if my family thought my interests odd at that time, but in measuring my life against theirs, in retrospect, it must have seemed rather peculiar.

When I went to Vietnam, I carried a couple of poetry anthologies with me. I continued to read poetry but was not writing it. I was in the information field and was doing newspaper work. When I came back from the war, I found myself enrolled in a poetry workshop at the University of Colorado, and I have been writing regularly ever since. The first poem I wrote when I felt I could call myself a "Poet" was called "Instructions for Building Straw Huts." I realized after writing that poem that a certain number of worlds had come together to coalesce in a kind of strange unity for me. The poem radiated with a number of surprises, and I realized that I wanted surprises in my work from then on. If I don't have surprises, poetry doesn't work for me. What gives my poetry its surprising element is that I have not systematically planned out in a directed way what I am going to say. It is a process of getting back to the unconscious. I am always writing—I am writing even when I am not facing a blank page. I feel that writers are like reservoirs of images. We take in that which is out there in order to at least understand that which is inside of us. In the poetry classes that I teach, I tell students to write everything down—not to think of the shape of the poem until the words are all down—and then to worry about revising, to be ready for the surprises, and to take them as gifts.

I feel like everything is urgent, which is just the way my life seems to go. So in terms of what ends up in my poetry, anything and everything is subject matter. Often one of the real problems in teaching creative writing, particularly to undergaduates, is that the students think there is something outside of themselves, so distant from their lives, that is a more proper subject matter. My tactic is to try and convince them that things that are very close to them are appropriate to write about—it doesn't have to be an experience in Italy or Japan. Many times people try to pull away from things that are close to them, but that is where the energy exists. We don't have to impose a superficial, invented subject matter in order to write.

There is automatically a psychological overlay for my poetry, as well as for who I am, when talking about blackness. I have never thought about the issue of blackness as subject matter for my poetry per se, but I suppose it has a lot to do with my perspective in terms of the shape of my emotional life. How I began to look at the world early on has a lot to do with the whole emotional shape of my adult artistic life, but I do not think that I would like to sit down and face the page, and say, "I am now going to write as a black man." I don't even entertain that thought, because I know who I am, and I don't have to face the mirror every day to remind myself. I've always accepted who I am and have hoped to let that be what directs my poetic vision.

I realize, by just going back and looking at folklore, that there have been tints all along of what we are dealing with today in terms of being black and male in our society today. Because there have always been certain figures in the community who we automatically categorize in what is often called "The Bad Nigger Syndrome." This mythical "bad nigger" is really a kind of phantom, because if we think in terms of folklore, he has no real power. If violence is power, then it is only in the context of the neighborhood in which it is committed. It is not clear whether black men have a sense of authentic power. In terms of my own experience, I had to sit down and have a talk with myself. It has not been so much about power for me as it has been about authorizing my sense of self. We are given all of these vivid pictures of individuals who do not have any authority, or semblance of power, which works as a kind of psychological warfare. We need to remove those stereotypical images from our psyche—I'm talking about our collective psyche.

It's hard for me to dissect imagination and reality because I realize that the two create a necessary merger. They are constantly fighting and reshaping each other, so there is a kind of imaginitive chemistry going on informed by the "truth." I like the fact that there is this organic, constantly changing chemistry going on beneath poetry, and the need to write it. There has to be a need to write—if there isn't a need, then everything else becomes artificial. There are things moving along in our imaginitive universes without us being able to define them or to put any kind of logical shape around them. Consequently, we want to control all of that mysterious activity. Ultimately, we have to get rid of the mechanism of control and place our lives in the hands of who we are. Without boundaries. It is a scary venture, but if it felt safe, it might become static or contrived. One has to realize that we only fill so much space. In filling that space, if there is any control involved, it is the control of one's ability to live in the moment.

It is difficult for me to write about things in my life that are very private, but I feel that I am constantly moving closer to my personal terrain—the idea of trying to get underneath who I am. I realize that we are all such complex human beings, and that there is a core in all of us that is composed of many layers. For me, and my writing, it is a process of removing those layers to understand what is at the core, and also realizing that I can incorporate all of those layers into a clarified idea of who I am. The layers become overlays in the place of obstructions. I know that I have helped to create the layers, despite who I am as a thinking human being. Many times I try to push aside the easier things to write about, like my daily observations, and come back to them later when there is more psychological debris to deal with. But I find both the more personal writing, as well as the more common, whimsical writing, to be very satisfying.

I have never purposely written a poem for a select group of people. Generally, I just find myself writing a poem. There are certain poems I can read to young black men and women, and automatically they grasp the language within the poetry. There are other poems that people have told me they had to reread a few times before they could actually understand it. I like the idea that the meaning of my poetry is not always on the surface, and that people may return to the work. I often don't like a poem in the first reading, but when I go back and read it again, there is a kind of growth that has happened within me as well as within the poem, and I become a participant rather than just a reader. I try to encourage this sort of participation in my own poetry—I try to create a space where a reader can come and participate in the meaning. This way, the poem doesn't necessarily mean one thing and allows the reader to be a cocreator of its meaning. A poem doesn't shut down after it is written, nor is there a resolution at its end, there is a kind of open-endedness that invites the reader to enter, and if there is a surface meaning, to help redirect the course of that meaning.

From

I APOLOGIZE FOR THE EYES
IN MY HEAD

The Music That Hurts

Put away those insipid spoons.
The frontal lobe horn section went home hours ago.
The trap drum has been kicked
down the fire escape,
& the tenor's ballad amputated.
Inspiration packed her bags.
Her caftan recurs in the foggy doorway
like brain damage; the soft piano solo of her walk
evaporates; memory loses her exquisite tongue,
looking for "green silk stockings with gold seams"
on a nail over the bathroom mirror.
Tonight I sleep with Silence,
my impossible white wife.

From
COPACETIC
Black String of Days

Tonight I feel the stars are out
to use me for target practice.
I don't know why
they zero in like old
business, each a moment of blood
unraveling forgotten names.
This world of dog-eat-dog
& anything goes.
On the black string of days
there's an unlucky number
undeniably ours.
As the Milky Way
spreads out its map
of wounds, I feel
like a snail on a salt lick.
What can I say? Morning's crow
poses on a few sticks, a cross
dressed in Daddy's work shirt—
how its yellow eyes shine.
It knows I believe
in small things.
I dig my fingers into wet dirt
where each parachute seed pod
matters. Some insect
a fleck of fool's gold.

I touch it,
a man asking for help
as only he knows how.

■

From
MAGIC CITY
Sugar

I watched men at Angola,
How every swing of the machete
Swelled the day black with muscles,
Like a wave through canestalks,
Pushed by the eyes of guards
Who cradled pump shotguns like lovers.
They swayed to a Cuban samba or Yoruba
Master drum & wrote confessions in the air
Saying *I been wrong*
But I'll be right someday.
I gazed from Lorenzo's '52 Chevy
Till they were nighthawks,
& days later fell asleep
Listening to Cousin Buddy's
One-horse mill grind out a blues.
We fed stalks into metal jaws
That locked in sweetness
When everything cooled down & crusted over,
Leaving only a few horseflies
To buzz & drive the day beyond
Leadbelly. At the bottom

Of each gallon was a glacier,
A fetish I could buy a kiss with.
I stared at a tree against dusk
Till it was a girl
Standing beside a country road
Shucking cane with her teeth.
She looked up & smiled
& waved. Lost in what hurts,
In what tasted good, could she
Ever learn there's no love
In sugar?

■

Yellow Dog Café

In a cerulean ruckus
Of quilts, we played house
Off the big room where
They laughed & slowdragged
Weekends. *The eagle flies
On Friday*. The jukebox pulsed
A rainbow through papery walls.
We were paid a dollar to guard
Each other. I was eight
& S.C. Mae fourteen,
As we experimented with
The devil. Mill workers
Changed money in the briny
Glow of bootleg, overpowered
By the smell of collards, catfish,
& candied yams. Granddaddy Gabriel

Worked the cash register
Beside his second wife, Rosie
Belle. I heard my mother
& father laugh like swimmers
Underwater. A raw odor
Of lilies & sweat filled the room;
My cousin's hands moved over me
Smooth & tough as a blues guitar.
Somebody swore they saw
A silhouette with a gasoline can
The night S.C. Mae ran away
With a woman's husband.
For weeks they sifted ashes
But the gutted studs & braces
Only leaned against the wind,
Weak as a boy & girl entwined
On the floor. That June
Granddaddy drove a busload
Up north: the growers paid him
A dollar a day for each pair of hands.
He wanted to rebuild those nights,
Their circle of blurred cards.
The bus grunted between orchards,
& by late August I had enough
Fire-blackened nickels & dimes
To fill a sock, but only a few pickers
Came back after a season of wine-stained
Greenbacks sewn inside coats
& taped to the soles of their feet.

NATHAN McCALL was ten years old when he first started playing childhood games with the neighborhood kids. By the time he turned fourteen, the games had become gang fights, gang rapes, and petty theft. At twenty years of age he was a father, a drug dealer, had shot a man, and faced a twelve-year prison sentence for armed robbery. McCall's best-selling autobiography, *Makes Me Wanna Holler: A Young Black Man in America*, chronicles his journey from a life on the streets to life in prison, where he transformed himself before going on to become a journalist at *The Washington Post*. The movie rights for McCall's life story have been optioned by Columbia Pictures. McCall is currently working on the film's screenplay, which will be directed by John Singleton. McCall lives in Washington, D.C.

FEEL THAT A BOOK IS MORE POWERFUL
than a gun could ever be. It's a much better get-off. If I get
mad at white folks . . . I can write something.

I push hard at writing for the results. And it's not strictly mone-
tary. I think a lot of people who may not have been inclined to
read my book (*Makes Me Wanna Holler*) will read it now that it
is on *The New York Times* best-seller list, and that is good. A lot
of people can't get past the first paragraph where I talk about one
particularly graphic and violent incident from my childhood.
When those people see that enough other people got past that
part—enough people to make the book a best-seller—then maybe
they'll give it another chance. I want white people to read the
book because I think that there is information in there that they
need to hear. The book gives white people a lot to chew on.

I didn't think of any particular audience when I was writing
the book. Now and then I would think about who might be reading it while I was simultaneously struggling with my writer's voice.
And at those times I was primarily thinking about the brothers. I
wanted to write a book that the brothers could pick up and read,
anytime, anywhere—in the joint, on the street, in college—and be
able to relate to in voice as well as in content. I had had a discussion with my editor early on about my voice, and whether or not it
would lose white readers. For example, whether or not I would
explain certain slang; if I said *joanin'*, would I have to explain that
joanin' is a form of verbally harassing someone?

My editor, who is white, was good as a devil's advocate and in
some ways reaffirmed my reasons for writing the book. In hearing
her question whether or not white people would understand the
language, it became more and more clear to me that my first con-

stituency was and still is black folks. If black folks don't know the exact meaning of the slang, they can pick it up contextually. I have often read things by white folks that I don't understand—I still don't know what a *schmuck* is—and I have to look those things up in the dictionary, and work at figuring out their meanings. I thought it would be good for white folks to do some work too. There are a lot of white folks who are eager to push me out there as some sort of Horatio Alger. Because if I get out there saying, "Yes! I did it myself! I pulled myself up by my bootstraps!" then the white folks are going to say, "If you did it, then all them other black folks can do it too." And that's going to absolve white folks of their responsibility to help us figure out the racial dilemma. Black people didn't create racism and violence by ourselves, and we can't solve it by ourselves.

I chose writing as a means to express my feelings and my life because really, what else is there? If I told a friend my story, how far would it get? Maybe to two or three more people? When I was locked up, one of the things that helped me to decide that I wanted to become a writer was this article that I ran across in the library. The article was about some conference that had been held in Europe where all these historians had gotten together to come up with a consensus about who was the most influential person in all of history. As I was reading the article, I started to guess at who that influential person might be, and I thought maybe it would be the prophet Muhammad. I figured that a lot of Europeans would probably think that it would be Jesus, but it was neither Jesus nor the prophet Muhammad. It was Gutenberg, the man who discovered movable type—the written word. I could talk my ass off until I'm blue in the face and maybe reach twenty or thirty people, but the written word is permanent. You can take a book and circulate that bad boy all over the world.

I haven't been able to read the book straight through since I finished writing it, but every now and then at readings or book signings, people will mention sections that make me want to go over and read them again. Sisters talk to me about the chapter on "Trains." A lot of sisters come up to me and say, "You know, I had a hard time with that chapter, my brother." One sister came up to me in Los Angeles and told me that she had had such a hard time with that chapter that she put the book down and wasn't going to read any more, but she had been encouraged to keep reading by another sister who had finished the book.

That was the most difficult chapter to write. I almost talked myself out of writing it. I started writing the book by saying, "I'm going to be brutally honest in the book, I'm not pulling any punches, nothing," and when I got to that chapter, it was almost too painful to think about as an adult. I had often thought about that part of my past and felt that I had confronted it squarely, but it felt different when I had to take it to another level of understanding and actually put it down on paper. Before, I didn't have to make a commitment to thinking about it—I could think about it and when it got to be too much, I could walk away from the thought. I never had to think about it in as much detail as I did when I wrote it down. And at that point, I couldn't walk away. I had to consider the sisters who were victims of those rapes—where they are now and whether or not they were able to recover, or if the damage was too traumatizing and irreparable. It will always haunt me. I'm the kind of person who likes to tie up loose ends—and that is an end I cannot tie up.

I remember there was this cat who I was in prison with—he and I used to rap a lot—and he told me that he had killed a man and had never gotten caught for it. He was in prison on another charge. He told me about how it happened and whatnot. And even though he was glad that he had gotten away, it was on him, you know? It was *with* him. And it would always be with him. He was like me in the joint, he was striving to get in touch with his humanity, so he was feeling things for the first time. When you're out there on that block in the 'hood, you learn to turn it off. By the time I got to prison, I wasn't *feeling* things in the same way that I feel things now. Because you just can't. You can't be out there and *feel*. Because if you do, you're a dead man. So the rapes that I talk about in the book, that I participated in during the earlier part of my life, are with me. And they will always be with me. There's no way that I could publicly apologize to all of those women. I think the best thing that I could have done is to write about it and put it out there.

The reason that I didn't go back on the streets when I got out of prison was because of the safety net I had at home with my parents. I truly believe that if I had not had that security, I would have ended up right back on the street. I saw so many brothers who got out at the same time I did—we were all on an even keel and were determined to do right—but as we began to face the hardships in terms of trying to start anew, that's when it became clear what we were up against. When I started looking for a job things got real hard because I have a felony record. Job hunting is expensive, and I eventually ran out of money. I was able to turn to my parents and say, "I'm flat broke and I need some help." Most of the cats who came out of prison with me didn't have that—when they started running out of money, they had no one to turn to. I had someone who could hold me up, and I knew it.

There is that one incident in the book when I had gotten out of prison and I'm sitting in front of that twenty-four-hour store, ready to rip it off—if at that moment I didn't feel that I had someone who I could go to and say, "Look, I'm out of money, *again*," I would have taken that store. I made the choice not to because I *had* the choice. It all boils down to available choices and the perception of those choices. Ultimately, the choice is always an individual choice—but who thinks in terms of the ultimate? It's easy to sit there and be philosophical about it if you have choices. I know that if I didn't have my folks—I don't give a damn where my head was—my logic would have been: Just this one, just this one hit to tide me over.

I'm much further along now than when I first stepped out of the joint. I feel like I could be anywhere now and be able to put it together. When I got out of the joint, I was dealing in theory—I hadn't lived much on the side of the fence that allows me to be in this conversation that we are having right now. It was all an experiment then. When reality started to set in, and I saw what I could do with the theory when it went into motion, then I knew I would never turn back.

It's not enough to preach to folks. Those who do turn back are in an environment where nothing in their reality is reinforcing what I'm trying to preach. Why should they believe what I am telling them? I can't tell some kid to go to college because it's great for him if he can't look around and see in his *immediate* environment someone who has been to college and has not only benefitted from it, but who is also an admirable person. It's just words until that kid can look around and see his reality reinforce those words. So I try to be very careful about preaching to kids.

When I do talk to young brothers, I try to challenge their notions on what manhood is and isn't. Young brothers are so entrenched in that manhood thing that the only way they can really think about transcending or changing their ways is if they are approached in a way that fits their definitions of manhood. 'Cause otherwise, brothers ain't goin' for it—they ain't goin' for it, you know? So I try to give them another way of looking at things. I say, "Look, I understand you wanna be bad, I wanna be bad too, I ain't never stopped wantin' to be bad, but I figured out a way to be badder than I was in the past. It's one thing to be bad out on that block, but it really doesn't take that much to pull a trigger. If you really wanna be bad, let's take on that white man. Let's cross the tracks and engage him with our minds." I don't know if it's going to work, but at least it offers another way to look at it. Truth be told, a lot of brothers are afraid of the white man. They'd kill a brother in a minute, but they scared of that white man. So if we try to use our knowledge instead of our violence, we may be able to alter that fear.

One of the chief barometers of manhood is whether or not you can stand up to the white man. When I was coming up, all I had to do was to look at my stepfather—who was a potential role model for manhood—and see him down on his knees, working in white people's gardens. No, uh-uh. That ain't gonna get it. Then I looked out on the corner of the block, and the brothers were out there posturing, stylin', jivin'—you know, *that* was manhood. Those guys *looked* like men to me. Again, we are talking about perception versus reality. Those guys out on the corner looked like they didn't take no shit off *nobody*. And that's what I wanted to be like. I was looking for a hero and never had to create one, because there were plenty standing out there on the corner of the block.

My stepfather is a hero to me now because I realize that he did what he had to do; if he had to bend, then he bent. I don't know if I could ever be that much of a man. And when I was twelve and thirteen, I wasn't thinking about doin' nobody's bending—I was looking for somebody who was standing tall. If I were twelve or thirteen *now*, I'm not sure that I would be able to find any role models in the mainstream who fit the definition of manhood that I clung to for so long, and that is still a natural inclination to maintain when you grew up or are growing up in the ghetto. I mean who you gonna look to? Jesse Jackson has been completely marginalized, and the Congressional Black Caucus is losing its voice. If I were twelve or thirteen now, I'd probably look to rappers Snoop Doggy Dog or Tupac too—'cause they're posturin', you know, standing tall. Snoop and Tupac represent some real black images, however misguided they may or may not be. Ain't that many Malcolms around, you know? The closest thing we have to Malcolm is Farrakhan. And I don't have to agree with everything Farrakhan is saying to know that he is standing tall.

The reality of manhood was the same when I was a young brother as it is now as an adult. Only my perceptions of it have changed. I'm not too old to have heroes and they still gotta stand tall. Could be a man or a woman. I understand now that you're not more of a man if you can fight or make a woman feel bad about herself. Although it may not be clear from my actions coming up, I was looking for a sense of integrity, a feeling of being free to do what I choose—unbought and unbossed. I didn't equate my integrity with how I related to women then, and now I do. Now I consciously try to keep abreast of women I admire. Eleanor Holmes Norton—she's bad. I like her demeanor, I like her style, I like her mind. Lani Guinier—bad. Maya Angelou—bad. As a whole, I think we need to actually pay more homage to women heroines. Because we have serious problems with misogyny in black culture.

The irony is that there are more sisters out there who are really bad than there are brothers. I think black women are stronger than black men. Let me tell you what—right now, I'm more inclined to believe that God is a woman. The Creator doesn't even have to be a gender, but if it is—it's gonna be a woman. I am convinced of that. It took me a long time to embrace that notion. I think that intelligence is about sensitivity and the ability to be in touch with your humanity. I had to learn how to be sensitive and understand human compassion philosophically before I could integrate it into my reality. Women seem to come into the world with that sensitivity and humanity already intact. I had to work really hard at having sensitivity come naturally to me. I prayed a lot to reach that point because I knew how crucial it was.

It's not women who are into the macho thing, or who need a definition of womanhood before they become women—being a woman is a foregone conclusion. Men are so concerned first about what our manhood is, then we are worried about how we're going to keep it because we're so afraid that someone is going to take it! I wonder how that became a process for men but not for women? And it is cross-cultural, it's not exclusive to black culture.

Some days my writing would flow all day and into the night. I tried hard to stay with it. I believe human beings embody the knowledge of the universe inside of us. Some of us unlock it and some of us don't. Anything that I wanted to put in the book, I discovered would come to me if I let it. In the initial phases of the book, I was trying to force that knowledge. Then I realized that if I was patient, it would come to me. After I got about midway through the book, I understood that if the words didn't come, I could get up and do something else for a while and just wait on the words. Just wait. Eventually it would come. I would sit down, and Pow! There it was. Journalism works against that discipline of waiting, because you write on demand whether it flows or not. I got very comfortable with the freedom of letting the words come when they were ready, and I'm not anxious to give that freedom up.

I don't know if I will attempt fiction writing as a medium. I feel that there is a lot of power in fiction writing, and that it is sometimes more true than nonfiction. I've learned more from fiction than I have from nonfiction. There is more flexibility in fiction. When I was locked up I wrote a lot of poetry. Journalism really saps that creative energy, so I haven't written much poetry in a while. I love poetry because I can write it down however it comes. In terms of flowing, poetry flows more than any form of writing. When I was in prison, I was so attuned to the flow of poetry that I could get up out of bed in the middle of the night and write a poem. The next day I would read it and feel as though I only needed to change one or two words. I like that. I also like the fact that you don't have to adhere to rules in poetry.

I think I broke a lot of rules in *Makes Me Wanna Holler.* I actually tried not to think about rules. I wanted to do some things that I didn't think anybody else had done—mainly just to bear the indiscriminate truth. Generally people are scared to lay it all out, especially men. Maybe this book was another manhood challenge for me. Writing requires that you be in touch with your humanity, and because women are more in touch with their humanity than men are, then writing may come across as a more feminine medium. But I don't think being in touch with your humanity is necessarily feminine—it is just that there are more women who are in touch with their humanity. Women have a monopoly on humanity! But humanity is not gender specific. And so neither is writing.

I feel like it's okay to have my life be public knowledge. I reached a point when I decided to write this book where I knew that nothing could destroy me. Because once you put everything out on the table, you have nothing to fear. I have nothing left to hide. The book is more than an autobiography, it's a piece of my soul. And I know what's in my soul. I know what I got inside.

From
MAKES ME WANNA HOLLER
Native Son

One night, the familiar sound of jangling keys echoed outside my new cellblock. I looked up and saw two white men walking briskly down the hallway toward the entrance. One was a jail guard. The other, walking a step or two ahead, was a tall, influential-looking man who appeared to be in his fifties. Wearing an expensive suit and a white shirt unbuttoned at the collar, the man looked like he had just ended a long, tiring business day. When the two reached the entrance, the guard opened the door, let the man inside, then closed and locked the gate. The man stood there for a long moment, sighed wearily, and scanned the room.

By now, everybody in the cellblock had turned from what they were doing to study the newcomer. There were a few other whites in the cellblock, but he was different from anybody I'd seen come through those gates. Everything in this man's dress and manner suggested that he came from the upper reaches of a world I had only read and talked about. He had that saunaed, pampered look about him and seemed to be the kind of white man who was unaccustomed to being inconvenienced, let alone locked up.

Apparently unnerved by the prisoners' glares, the newcomer turned around, leaned his head against the cell bars, and stared out into the empty hallway. The guard returned minutes later and handed him a mattress and a set of crumpled jail clothes. A white inmate walked over and steered the new man to an empty bunk. They chatted quietly a moment, then the inmate walked away, leaving him there to get settled. I learned later from that inmate that my initial take on the newcomer was on the money: An executive at some high-powered business firm, the man had been busted for a white-collar rip-off.

He sat on his bunk and looked around, bewildered. I could tell by the tortured expression on his fleshy face that this was his worst nightmare. For him, the world had turned upside down and inside out: Black people were in the majority, and they ran things; white people were in the minority, and they were oppressed. Clearly, he had never dreamed he'd spend a minute even passing through our world.

He stayed anchored to his bunk the remainder of the night and part of the next day. He was still glued there that afternoon when we gathered in the dayroom to begin our group therapy session. Just as we were about to start, a guy called Titty Head (his head was shaped like a woman's breast) shouted to the newcomer: "Yo, Mr. Executive! I know you ain't used to bein' told what to do, but you gotta bring your pompous ass out here just like everybody else!"

The man's pasty white face turned beet red. With all eyes on him, he rose, walked slowly out of the sleeping area, and took a seat at one of the steel tables. We started the session, sending inmates to the hot seat. After several guys had spoken, Titty Head turned to the newcomer. "Okay, Mr. Executive, it's your turn to bare your soul."

I knew what Titty Head was doing. Everybody knew. He was taking a rare chance to strike back at somebody who represented the very system that made his life hell. This was his once-in-a-life-time shot, a chance to get even, and he intended to milk it for all it was worth. We asked the man a lot of offensive, deeply personal questions, and he responded, trying to hide his resentment at having to answer to people he probably considered beneath himself. Titty Head in particular hit him with a lot of questions framed more in the form of accusations. "I bet you dog niggahs out on the job every chance you get, don't you?!"

Throughout the grilling, the few other whites in the cellblock kept quiet, taking care not to jeopardize their own fragile safety. I sat watching, enjoying the *hell* out of it, loving the sight of a powerful white man squirming in the clutches of powerless blacks. I suspected he felt indicted by his whiteness as never before, and I hoped he felt at that moment the same way I'd felt for much of my life: like an alien in a hostile world where he couldn't win; like the victim of recurring injustices against which there were no appeals.

We kept the newcomer on that hot seat and fucked with his head for hours. When the meeting ended, he retreated to his bunk, humiliated, and sulked the rest of the day. The following day, the brothers rode him some more, on the hot seat and off. They looked him up and down in the shower like he was a piece of shit and barked orders at him, reminding him constantly that his life was now subject to a whole new set of rules.

After a few days, the newcomer got out on bond. When the guard called his name and yelled, "Pack your bags!," he nearly *flew* to the gate and didn't even bother to gather most of his belongings. As he left, he looked through the bars one final time at the thirty or so black men eyeing him. His lips parted as though he were about to say something, but he kept quiet and walked on away.

Whites in general caught hell in jail, especially in my new cellblock, which was less disciplined and far rowdier than the other one I'd been in. White junkies, whose drug dealings had often taken them to inner-city spots, did well because they'd grown comfortable around blacks. But that was less the case with those sheltered, smug whites, such as that businessman we'd put through hell. They wore their racial fears and prejudices on their sleeves.

At night, when the lights went out, those whites who couldn't hold their own were harrassed, sexually and otherwise, by the wolves. One morning, I woke up and saw a young, long-haired white guy sitting on his bunk, staring dejectedly at the floor. His lips were swollen and his eyes were black and puffy from an apparent thumping he'd taken the night before. He was taken to the dispensary, then placed in protective custody. I heard through the rumor mill that he'd been raped and beaten by a few wolves while everyone else was asleep. Eventually, several brothers were fingered and charged with the rape.

Those and similar incidents involving whites reminded me that our little saying in Cavalier Manor rang true everywhere, especially in jail: "Payback is a motherfucka."

There were moments in that jail when the confinement and heat nearly drove me mad. At those times, I desperately needed to take my thoughts beyond the concrete and steel. When I felt restless tension rising, I'd try anything to calm it. I'd slap-box with other inmates until I got exhausted, or play chess until my mind shut down. When all else failed, I'd pace the cellblock perimeter like a caged lion. Sometimes, other inmates fighting the temptation to give in to madness joined me, and we'd pace together, round and round, and talk for hours about anything that got our minds off our misery.

I eventually found a better way to relieve the boredom. I noticed that some inmates broke the monotony by volunteering for certain jobs in the jail. Some mopped the halls, and others worked in the dispensary or the kitchen. When the inmate librarian was released from jail, I asked for and was given his job. I began distributing books on the sixth floor as part of a service provided by the Norfolk Public Library. A couple of times a week, I pushed a cart to each cellblock and let inmates choose books and place orders for literature not on the cart. I enjoyed the library work. It gave me a chance to get out into the halls and walk around, and to stick my face to the screens on the floor windows and inhale fresh air.

Beyond the short stories I'd read in high school, I hadn't done much reading. Naturally, while working for the library, I leafed through more books than I normally would have. One day, shortly after starting the job, I picked up a book featuring a black man's picture on the cover. It was titled *Native Son*, and the author was Richard Wright. I leafed through a few pages in the front of the book, and couldn't put it down. The story was about a confused, angry young black man named Bigger Thomas, whose racial fears lead him to accidentally suffocate a white woman. In doing so, he delivers himself into the hands of the very people he despises and fears.

I identified strongly with Bigger and the book's narrative. He was twenty, the same age as me. He felt the things I felt, and, like me, he wound up in prison. The book's portrait of Bigger captured all those conflicting feelings—restless anger, hopelessness, a tough facade among blacks and a deep-seated fear of whites—that I'd sensed in myself but was unable to express. Often, during my teenage years, I'd felt like Bigger—headed down a road toward a destruction I couldn't ward off, beaten by forces so large and amorphous that I had no idea how to fight back. I was surprised that somebody had written a book that so closely reflected my experiences and feelings.

I read that book every day, and continued reading by the dim light of the hall lamps at night, while everyone slept. On that early morning when I finished reading *Native Son*, which ends with Bigger waiting to go to the electric chair, I broke down and sobbed like a baby. There is one passage that so closely described how I felt that it stunned me. It is a passage where a lawyer is talking to Bigger, who has given up hope and is waiting to die:

You're trying to believe in yourself. And every time you try to find a way to live, your own mind stands in the way. You know why that is? It's because others have said you were bad and they made you live in bad conditions. When a man hears that over and over and looks about him and sees that life is bad, he begins to doubt his own mind. His feelings drag him forward and his mind, full of what others say about him, tells him to go back. The job in getting people to fight and have faith is in making them believe in what life has made them feel, making them feel that their feelings are as good as others'.

After reading that, I sat up in my bunk, buried my face in my hands, and wept uncontrollably. I cried so much that I felt relieved. It was like I had been carrying those feelings and holding in my pain for years, keeping it pushed into the back of my mind somewhere.

I was unaccustomed to dealing with such deep feelings. Occasionally, I'd opened up to Liz, but not a lot. I was messed up inside, empty and afraid, just like Bigger. *Native Son* confirmed for me that my fears *weren't* imagined and that there were rational reasons why I'd been hurting inside.

I developed through my encounter with Richard Wright a fascination with the power of words. It blew my mind to think that somebody could take words that described exactly how I felt and put them together in a story like that. Most of the books I'd been given in school were about white folks' experiences and feelings. I spent all that time learning about damned white folks, like my reality didn't exist and wasn't valid to the rest of the world. In school, the only time we'd really focused on the lives of black people was during Black History Week, which they set aside for us to learn the same old tired stories about Booker T. Washington and a few other noteworthy, dead black folks I couldn't relate to. But in *Native Son* I found a book written about a plain, everyday brother like myself. That turned me on in a big way and inspired me to look for more books like that.

Before long, I was reading every chance I got, trying to more fully understand why my life and the lives of friends had been so contained and predictable, and why prison—literally—had become a rite of passage for so many of us. I found books that took me places I'd never dreamed I could travel to and exposed me to a range of realities that seemed as vast as the universe itself.

Once, after reading a book of poems by Gwendolyn Brooks, I wrote to her, not really expecting to receive a reply. She wrote me back and sent me an inspirational paperback of hers titled *Aloneness*. I was thrilled that a well-known black writer like her had taken the time to respond to me.

I was most attracted to black classics, such as Malcolm X's autobiography. Malcolm's tale helped me understand the devastating effects of self-hatred and introduced me to a universal principle: that if you change your self-perception, you can change your behavior. I concluded that if Malcolm X, who had also gone to prison, could pull his life out of the toilet, then maybe I could, too.

Up to that point, I'd often wanted to think of myself as a baad nigger, and as a result, I'd tried to act like one. After reading about Malcolm X, I worked to get rid of that notion and replace it with a positive image of what I wanted to become. I walked around silently repeating to myself, "You are an intelligent-thinking human being; you are an intelligent-thinking human being . . . ," hoping that it would sink in and help me begin to change the way I viewed myself.

Malcolm X made his conversion through Islam. I'd seen Muslims selling newspapers and bean pies on the streets, but I didn't know anything about their religion. I was drawn to Christianity, mostly because it was familiar. I hadn't spent much time in church. It seemed that all they did in churches I'd been to was learn how to justify suffering at the hands of white folks. But now there were Christian ministers active at the jail, and I became interested. They came around about once a week and talked to inmates through the bars, prayed with them and read Scripture. I started talking with them about God and about life in general.

It wasn't hard to accept the possibility that there was a higher force watching over me. When I looked back at my life, I concluded that there had been far too many close calls—times when I could have offed somebody or gotten killed myself—for me to believe I had survived solely on luck. I wondered, *Why didn't that bullet strike Plaz in the heart when I shot him? Why didn't I pull the trigger on that McDonald's manager when he tried to get away? And why wasn't I on the corner the night my stick partners were shot?* Unable to come up with rational answers to those questions, I reasoned that God must have been pulling for me.

My interest in spiritual things also came from a need to reach out at my most powerless point and tap into a higher power, something beyond me and, at the same time, within me. I longed for a sense of wholeness that I had never known but sensed I was entitled to. I set out to learn more about my spiritual self, and I began exploring the Bible with other inmates who held Bible studies some nights in the cellblock.

At some point, I also got a library copy of the book—*As a Man Thinketh*—that Reverend Ellis had given me in college. I immediately understood what he had been trying to get across: that thinking should be an *active* process that, when cultivated, can change a person's behavior, circumstances, and, ultimately, his fate.

When I first started reading, studying, and reflecting on the information I got from books, I had no idea where it all might lead. Really, it didn't matter. I was hungry for change and so excited by the sense of awakening I glimpsed on the horizon that the only thing that mattered was that I had made a start. I often recited the Scripture that Reverend Ellis had given me to read before I was sentenced: "Everything works together for the good of those that love God, for those who are called according to His purpose." *If that's true*, I thought, *maybe I can get something positive out of this time in prison*. It sure didn't seem like it. But it made me feel better just thinking it might be possible.

CARYL

PHILLIPS

CARYL PHILLIPS was born in St. Kitts, West Indies, in 1958 and moved with his family to England that same year. He was brought up in Leeds and educated at Oxford University in England. He has written numerous scripts for film, theater, radio, and television. His nonfiction book, *The European Tribe,* won the 1987 Martin Luther King Memorial Prize. Phillips is the author of five novels, which include the critically acclaimed *Cambridge* (1992) and his most recent work, *Crossing the River* (1994). Phillips has lectured in several countries, including Sweden, Germany, and Ghana. In 1992 he was the recipient of the Guggenheim Fellowship. He is currently a professor of English and writer-in-residence at Amherst College in Amherst, Massachusetts, while maintaining homes in both London and St. Kitts.

WRITING IS NOT AT ALL like talking for me; talk is cheap, writing is serious.

I began writing plays in 1979, my last year of college. It had perhaps been a dream to write prose at that time, but I was a playwright for four or five years before I wrote anything that I was willing to call prose.

I had always been interested in the arts—I had directed plays in school and was quite interested in film as well. I was growing up in England, so if I wanted to be a director, there wasn't really a canon of work by black people that I could draw upon. There were no Lorraine Hansberrys or Jimmy Baldwins or August Wilsons; we didn't have black playwrights who were getting produced. We didn't even have a deep body of black actors. So I had to consider that if I was to be a play director, I would be forever servicing the work of white people, which is not a bad thing, but I knew that those plays would not reflect my life. As a young person who wanted to be involved in the arts, particularly in the performing arts, there was an onus on me to get to writing the material I was talking about there being none of. And that is how I began to write.

My yearning to write prose was fueled by two things: the independence that prose writing provided, and the permanence of it. Writing plays for a black cast in Britain meant that I would have my play produced once and that would be the end of that. I had a very strong feeling that there were probably a lot of people who would have liked to see one of my plays and who would have gotten a lot out of it, but if they weren't in that one small town on that one night, they would never see it. The plays of white playwrights would continue showing and would live and breathe and appear in several different cities. That never happened for my plays. The theaters that would show my plays would pat themselves on the back for producing a "black play" that season, but the play would only run for four weeks and then we would all go back to waiting tables. So I wanted to write something that would run for more than one season, and that would be accessible to more than the handful of people who showed up for that one season.

In 1984 I delivered a manuscript of prose writing to a publisher. I had been writing prose on my own all the time, I just hadn't been showing it to anyone. It was my own private obsession, and I never had any intention of revealing it until I was good and ready. The manuscript that I delivered was a novel, which is the only medium in writing beyond playwriting that I have ever been interested in. I knew that I was not talented at short stories because I don't read them, which was a fairly decent hint that I wouldn't be able to write them—we don't have architects who don't look at houses. One is effective in his work by going and looking at what it is that one is meant to create. One must take notes and take pictures before the imagination kicks in to create something original.

I have now written five novels that have been published and am pleased to say that the process of discovery in my writing is still fresh. The characters in my novels don't ever come out of nowhere—they are always rooted in some sort of social context. Usually research in a general area produces characters for my novels. If I am reading a book that is about a particular period in history and a character steps out and appeals to me, then I will continue to pursue that character. For example, I am very interested in Haiti, which doesn't mean anything in terms of a novel until somebody in a Haitian context begins to fascinate me. The more I read, the more I am looking for a character to whom I can lend some life, spirit, and voice. I've never had the experience of a voice or a person appearing to me devoid of a specific social context. Playwriting is very voice controlled—it's all dialogue. So sometimes one line of dialogue can lead me into the exploration of a character, which doesn't really happen with prose. In prose, I rely so much on painting the scene; I need to provide all of the sociological, historical, political, and cultural information, which is an intriguing exploit.

Keeping a character alive with only the knowledge of that character's social context involves a tremendous amount of faith. If a character has entrusted his or her story to me, I just have to hope that he or she will keep talking. There isn't much else I can do. As soon as I start imposing my own thoughts and voice upon the character in a heavy-handed way, the audience can tell that they are being led by the nose. I really don't know how the development of a character's life happens. Some characters will speak to me with an authority and a clarity that strikes me as true—if I knew how this happened, I would be writing four or five novels a year. I wish somebody would tell me how to do that, but no one has, so the question of the writer's relationship with his characters is a continuous one for me. I remain totally dependent on the character's social construct in order to get to know him or her, which can be a very frustrating process.

I often think the very popular novelists who are able to turn out four or five novels a year may be violating the authority of character because many of those novels are plot driven. Their characters are two-dimensional because the author has not waited for the character to fully present him or herself. For literary novelists, the deal is character. The problem is that when a writer puts a character before a plot, or when the plot is character driven, he becomes dependent upon the character's unpredictability. Which stands to reason, as human beings are unpredictable—they'll drive you around the bend, and characters are no different. When I want a character to jump, he or she won't jump. When I want a character to say boo, he or she won't say boo. It's like having a cat rather than a dog.

Between books I don't do anything but read and research ideas that may pop into my head. I have a research assistant who will research and collect material for me. I'll read the material, and when things begin to cook in my mind, I tend to go away. I'll go away to some far-off place and write a very fast first draft in longhand, take a break for a few weeks, and then the real hard part begins: turning that first draft into something that even vaguely resembles the English language. That process can take four or five months. For the very final draft I usually go and live in a hotel somewhere for about two or three weeks, and try to knock the thing into shape. After that, I won't write anything for at least a year.

The final draft of writing has taken me to Spain, Thailand, Cuba, France, Scotland—all over the place. I like hotels because there isn't anyone to bug me, and I don't have to clean up. It's neutral space for just me and my imagination. There is nothing to distract me unless I am particularly interested in watching *Home Alone 2* on the cable network. I am forced to sit there in a hotel room somewhere with only my characters for company. The more expensive the hotel, the better as well, because I am thinking: I can't afford this, what am I playing at here? That soon gets me back to my writing desk. The spur of financial shame around the corner is good incentive.

I teach a fiction class and a literature class one semester a year at Amherst College, which still allows me to go away when I need to. Next week I'm going to the Bahamas because I am meant to finish a screenplay and I know I won't finish it if I stay here freezing in this bloody cold winter. I enjoy teaching, though. I first started teaching as a writer-in-residence at the University of Mysore, in southern India, in 1987, and then went on to be the writer-in-residence at the University of Stockholm in Sweden. These were my first two formal experiences teaching, and I found that I really like working with students because it forces my own mind to think more deeply about writing and reading.

I went to college myself at Oxford University, and I knew I wasn't going back after that to do any of that fancy postgraduate stuff. I was happy to get out of Oxford as a relatively conscious, young black man. If I'd stayed around any longer, Lord knows what would've happened to me. I consider myself a part of the academy in the sense that I am a professor of English, but the politics within the academy don't mean that much to me. When I first started teaching at Amherst I was appalled at how restrictive and small-minded their world was, but I have always rested in the fact that I don't live here, and I don't have to live here. I have a house in England and I have a house in Saint Kitts, so it's not as if I *keep* anything here in the States. There is nothing on the shelves in my office here at Amherst. Whenever I get on the plane back to London, my bags are full because I bring all of my papers and books with me. I do research in the States and I teach here, but I don't live here.

The transience doesn't bother me. London is my primary home, and I make at least three or four phone calls there daily. As long as my mother and my siblings live there, London will be my home. The promiscuity of the sort of traveling that I have been doing over the past ten years or so makes a plane ride from Boston to London feel like jumping on a bus to get from one town to the next. I do it so often that I have my own routine and I know exactly what to do, it's all second nature now; changing monies and credit cards from American to British and what have you. I don't even get culture shock anymore. I don't arrive at Heathrow or at Logan or at the Caribbean and think: Where the hell am I? The only culture shock I ever get is from American TV. If I haven't been in America for a couple of months, I forget quite how absurd American television is. I watch "Love Connection" in utter disbelief.

I have always thought that if I were ever to leave Amherst I would also leave the States, so it is an interesting question about whether "here" means Amherst or the States in general. I appreciate what I have at Amherst, and I don't anticipate leaving. I also feel that the longer I stay, the better my relationship is with the States. It is a productive relationship, but certainly not always easy. While I may speak like Alistair Cooke, I look like Rodney King—so I'm as vulnerable to getting beat up as any black man in America is.

At first coming to America was a gig, but I have come to develop an interest in America that I didn't have originally. I consider America to be a very fertile and stimulating environment for writers. My alternatives for semipermanent geographic stimulus are these: the Caribbean is beautiful, but I would die of boredom if I lived there—how many palm trees can you look at? White beaches are terrific, terrific, terrific—but could somebody just talk to me about a book? There isn't enough intellectual stimulation for me to live there for any great length of time. Having grown up in Europe, I am accustomed to a consistent intellectual exchange. The other alternative is Britain, and to be quite honest I don't find Britain stimulating enough for a writer's mind. The British have a sort of anal retentive, cool chic about themselves. They think that it is bad form to use the term "intellectual"—that it is pretentious to call yourself an intellectual. But there is nothing pretentious or shameful about discussing books and art in a serious manner. I find that people in America discuss books, art, ideas, and films in a serious and dedicated manner, which is why I think many writers from all over the world end up living and working here for at least part of the time.

My experience as a black British man in the States has certainly been informative. Although Amherst is too refined to admit that racism exists on campus—it's like an ugly term that would spoil the dinner party if mentioned—I taught at NYU last semester, which was an environment where all the ills and evils of racism, class oppression, and underdevelopment were impinged upon me every time I walked across the campus. Beneath the veneer of the emergence of middle-class black America is a degree of acute underdevelopment that is very disturbing. The polarization within the black community between those who have and those who have not is very frightening. I don't really feel separate from the experience, but I also don't fully understand it because I've not been here long enough. I understand it intuitively, because while the race relations here in America do not exactly parallel those in Britain, I still grew up in a racist society. I'm reluctant to make the analogy at all because Americans have had a more disturbing relationship with black people, and for much longer than the British. However, because racism does not stop to make many distinctions, in America, I get the same looks and the same treatment, and when I open my mouth and speak with a British accent, people often think I'm trying to put one over. So I am very aware of the climate here, but much of my understanding of it has come from my black students. They teach the process of being black in America, and I teach the process of writing.

The first thing that I try to get my students to understand is that they'd better present their work properly—double spaced, page numbers, and all that, which usually takes about two weeks. And then I try to get them to take responsibility for the fact that we are all screwed up to some degree, which is why people write. I don't want any stories about little bunnies hopping around the field, I want to know what your problem is. No one takes a writing class unless they have something to say. If you've not got anything to say, why write? We spend a lot of time doing exercises that will instill trust among the students, because no one is going to spill the beans about their alcoholic mother or their father who just came out gay if they are not in a trusting environment. After we have created some sort of bond in the class, I encourage the students to take responsibility for their lives and to then understand the all-important thing, which is that good writing comes out of a sense of having something to say.

There has never really been any subject that has been difficult for me to write about. Most subjects demand accountability and sensitivity, but nothing has ever frightened me away. Sometimes I will include my own emotionality—my hang-ups and my fears—in my novels, but if I've got any good sense, I disguise it as best I can. What the reader can get through my writing about me as an author is up to him or her. That sort of deconstruction has little to do with the actual writing. It isn't so much through style that I divert the reader's attention from the autobiographical tendencies that may appear in my work, as it is character focus. There's no sense in having a fancy style of writing if I'm going to write about a character named Phillip Caryl, who is a thirty-five-year-old, educated, British black man. I consider style to be more deeply wedded to the prose, to the actual arrangement of sentences and to the perspective that the writer takes. It is much more effective to start with an entirely fictitious character and then to use my style of writing to tell a story that allows some space between my autobiographical eye and the actual craft of writing so that I can then dare to imagine.

As Eudora Welty said, "Dare to do with your bag of fears." I like the daring and I like the doing. It is a matter of craft to take your own bag of fears and to then turn it into something comprehensible to others. That is what writing is about. And that is what I dare to do.

From

CROSSING THE RIVER

Saint Paul's River, Liberia
Oct. 2nd, 1840

Dear Father,

I trust that these few hasty lines which I set down with respect find you in good health and fine spirits. Why your heart remains hard against me is a mystery which has caused me emotions of great distress. But so it must be. I can never guide your hand. I was greatly disappointed on the arrival of the last emigrant vessel by not receiving a single line from you. You chose to comment, in your only letter to this date, that you still have affection. But why do I not receive letters more often? I am so situated that I cannot see every vessel that comes on the coast, but my name and settlement are broadly known in this region. I like this place very well, but my greatest desire is that I may see you once more in this world. I have followed your counsel as much as possible. You need not be afraid that I shall forget or neglect them.

Did I tell you of my partiality to a young woman hereabouts? After a short courtship I put my addresses to her, and I expect to be somewhat true to her till I die. We were married on the first of March, she being a native woman, and one of the best in Africa. She faithfully discharges the office of mother to a child I possess by another, less successful, connection, and she remains an industrious woman who performs all the duties relative to house-keeping, including making clothes for her *family*. This *family*, above whom I reign as head, join me in sending love to their good father whom they have never seen. My son, whom I have taken the liberty of naming Edward in the hope that he might emulate your esteemed self, will soon be in need of materials to help speed his skills in reading and writing. You will therefore send me something. Anything you may choose to send will be acceptable, and the sum of three hundred dollars, being of no consequence to a man of your wealth, would suffice. I would be very thankful for some newspapers, and if you wish I will send to you a few of ours. I hope, dear Father, that you will send me a few working tools such as axes and hoes, for the like are very useful, but very hard to get here.

The fever in these parts is not so bad now as it used to be, for it would seem that the older the place gets, and the more it is cultivated, the better the fever is. Having long passed through the acclimatizing process, and having watched others do so with equal success, I am glad that I can say that I love this country more than I did at first. The seasons here remain quite different from those in my old country, yet the weather seems to get cooler. This year we have been blessed with little rain, and the sun has parched up most of all of the crops in the fields, so if you would be so kind as to send me out something, I would feel much obliged. Anything, I do not mind what it is, for I feel sure that it will make a valuable contribution.

Farming is now our main occupation, the numbers at the mission school having fallen off in a dramatic manner. I have my fields planted with potatoes, arrowroot, cassava and considerable corn. In addition, I have a large number of cotton bushes, and a variety of other vegetables. I have also planted a large piece in rice, and together with the natives work from morning till sunset clearing and planting. I should be much obliged to you if you would send me a mill, for I have tried to cut a stone for that purpose, but found it beyond me. I am not in such a prosperous situation as might be expected, for it remains difficult to exchange produce for foreign produce, and besides, we make up just enough to sustain us from starvation. I have fowls in plenty, of all kinds. I have also hogs and goats. My horned cattle are only now beginning to increase, and some of the more skilled natives have, under my influence, made fences to secure them. They would, before this, often run out into the woods where they would quickly become lost. Keeping this rich land in order, and clean of grass and weeds, is my main task. But any man who will use common industry can raise much that he will eventually employ.

If, dear Father, these lines should find you in the land of the living, I will be more than glad to hear from you. I have written many letters to you at different times across the breadth of the last few years, and yet you seem reluctant to engage with me. I have come to the conclusion that you have repudiated me for reasons that perhaps owe their origins to some form of shame. Is there perhaps someone who has poisoned your mind against me? If these lines should find you in health, please return me an answer by the shortest way. My pleas with you to aid me, on behalf of all of this settlement, have been ill-received, for you have made nothing available to ease my present circumstances. Like all new countries, this is a very hard one, and some kindness on your part would have been pleasing to me. Should you have chosen to send me seeds of all description, I would have gladly made some use of them. I have given you full accounts of this place, so you can be in no doubt as to the often troubling nature of affairs hereabouts. That you have chosen to ignore my request that I might once more visit America to pay respects to my departed mother, and to cast my eyes upon old friends, has caused my heart to suffer in a great deal of pain. I have little opportunity for intercourse with familiar emigrants in these parts, for most of those who know of you are scattered all about the country, some few up here, but most down in the capital. So daily I wonder about those names across the water who, hearing no news, I constantly fear may have already departed this life.

Only last week I chanced to go into Monrovia in order that I might visit with old friends, both white and black. But not only could I not discern any news, it would appear that my present domestic arrangements have caused some offense to those who would hold on to America as a beacon of civilization, and an example of all that is to be admired. Are we not in Africa? This is what I constantly asked of the blacks. But it appeared they felt I merely sought to justify my *native* style of living. I counter-rallied and made it plain that I have nothing to justify, for amongst the emigrants I am indisputably the proudest holder of my race, but I soon found myself effectively shunned by my fellow Americans, many of whom privately mock African civilization whilst outwardly aping the fashion and posture of persons returned home. I realized that it would be beneficial for my health were I to cease conversation, withdraw, and return for ever to the safety of my Saint Paul's River settlement.

Sad to report, but before my retreat from the capital I was able to ascertain that these days the chief topic of conversation is that ancient immovable, slavery. Hardly a week passes on this coast of Africa without some report of a sea-bound slaver, and its unfortunate cargo, who have been afforded protection by the unfurling of the Star Spangled Banner. Without the hoisting of this emblem, the British man-of-wars would quickly, and happily, take these ships captive and liberate their black inhabitants. To most colored men, who reside here in liberty, and would expect liberty to encompass all of Africa, this dark land of our forefathers, this American protectionism is a disgrace to our dignity, and a stain on the name of our country. The hoisting of some other banner would be scarcely less insulting, but that they choose to sport our national flag, this is surely too much. But sadly, there is still more to be said on this subject of slavery. It appears that slave-dealers are establishing slave factories within the territory of Liberia, cunningly situating them further down the coast in the hope of avoiding prying eyes. The Governor recently ordered one such villain away, telling him he had no right to deal in slaves in that territory, and instructing him under threat of penalty that he must remove his factory in so many days. However, contrary to his agreement, he would not do so, and so the factory was broken up and forty puncheons of rum turned loose on the ground. There are those in Monrovia who profit handsomely from this *business*, and who would choose to ignore the existence of such evil deeds and their correction, but the problems of slavery continue to plague us, yes, even here in the bosom of liberty.

The rains are still with us, and the sky continues to open its heart and shed tears upon all the known earth. Master, you took me into your house as a young boy and instructed me in the ways of civilized man. Under your tutelage, I acquired whatever rude skills I now possess in the art of reading and writing, and more besides. Why have you forsaken me? There are many things I cannot discuss with my native wife, for it would be improper for her to share with me the memories of what I was before. I am to her what she found here in Africa. If this is to be goodbye, then let it be with love and respect in equal portion. I must close these hasty lines by saying I remain your affectionate son.

Nash Williams

DARRYL PINCKNEY

D ARRYL PINCKNEY was born in Indianapolis, Indiana, in 1953. Educated at Columbia University, he has been a Hodder Fellow at Princeton University and a recipient of grants from the Ingramm-Merrill, Whiting, and Guggenheim foundations. A visiting scholar at Harvard University, Pinckney is a frequent contributor to *The New York Times Book Review,* among other publications. He has collaborated with Heiner Muller on the text for Robert Wilson's *The Forest* and adapted Virginia Woolf's *Orlando,* also for a Robert Wilson production. Pinckney's novel *High Cotton* (1992) received a *Los Angeles Times* Book Prize and the Harold D. Vursell Memorial Award for distinguished prose from the American Academy of Arts and Letters.

I DON'T KNOW WHAT I THINK until I see it on the page. I started writing in college when I decided that I wanted to make a life as a writer. I had always written—the usual juvenile sorts of things: the school newspaper; bad plays; tormented diaries; the worst poems; things like that.

I kept a journal growing up not because I thought that it would be read by anyone ever, but as a way of examining certain parts of my life, whatever life meant then. Writing that is autobiographical is common in youth, because your experience of the world is rather limited and everything is an immediate transcription of your experience. Then, too, the kind of black literature that I was introduced to at an early age was autobiographical: Frederick Douglass, Richard Wright, and James Baldwin.

I had trouble getting out of Indiana, but in the end I went to college in New York because, as Elizabeth Hardwick once said, Manhattan is the capital of the twentieth century. Meeting writers in New York made me see writing as a real possibility. I learned about writing first from my peers. At that time, Columbia was having trouble competing with other schools to admit certain kinds of students. There was this sense that the admission policy was—if you were weird, you were in. Consequently, there were a lot of very interesting students at Columbia.

There were writers who would come to Columbia as visiting professors. I remember Kenneth Koch's stanza class was rather infamous—as in difficult. By the time you'd written one hundred imitations of a Spenserian stanza, you had a fair idea of what it was, or you should have had. And David Shapiro also taught there. He was very young for a teacher, and so there was this conspiratorially avant-garde atmosphere in his classroom. Meeting writers and forming friendships opened up the city's cultural landscape for me. And then I took a writing class with Elizabeth Hardwick. It changed my life. She's the Nadia Boulanger of American literature. That class had a tremendous influence on my ideas about writing because she told me that I was not a poet. I'd been writing what I thought was poetry. The point is that, instead of expression, which I wanted to do a lot of in no particular form, I learned discipline in that class. And I also learned how important it is to read; that you learn to write not by writing, but by reading. I realized that while I might have been trying to imitate Sylvia Plath or Leroi Jones or Robert Hayden, I was still imitating other writers and not putting in what was necessary to make the work my own.

Hardwick taught me to find the joy of writing in revision. The first draft of anything I write always seems to me as if it had been written by a fool. Not "seems"—my first drafts *are* written by a fool. After I get it down and can start to work it over, I feel more engaged and more passionate about the writing life. I do know some writers for whom writing it all down is the last part of composition; they are able to compose in their heads before it goes down on the page. I certainly can't compose in my head. I do get lines and images that I want to pursue, but in that sense my head is more like a notebook.

If I have the first line and the last line of a chapter, or of a paragraph, then I can slowly fill in the rest. If I can't continue from the first line, if there is no flow or seepage, then I know that there is something wrong with the tone or the attitude, that or I'm not telling the truth, not bringing out what I really mean. Writing is a question of form and language and what the best way is to get it all out. I just have to trust myself. If I can get started, I will sit there until I am finished. That is something I had to learn the hard way. I have to trust that I will have enough time to say what I want to say, and I have to remind myself that not everything needs to happen in the first paragraph. The difficult part for me is making myself start.

When I talk about problems, with tone, attitude, and telling the truth, what I mean is that I must be careful not to be too high-minded; not to give into a provincialism that says "real literature" is at a certain pitch of ambition, or of thought, or of language. I have a tendency to be mannered, wrongly poetic. When I am trying to hide something, my voice comes across as empty, hollow. Whenever I think about why I am doing this or that, there is always the very high-minded reason, the self-congratulatory justification. But the truth is always in the very low reason, the more humble way of looking at things. There is a balance between the two, but the expression in my writing should go toward the lower, more realistic and fertile way of reasoning; the line of thought that helps you to discover another line of thought.

After college, I wrote a novel that was so bad I lost my nerve about writing. I can't even remember what it was about. I then thought about something Mary McCarthy said about young writers trying to make their way—that one of the things they could do was to write book reviews. So I wrote a review of Gayl Jones's novel *Corrigidora*, sent it somewhere, and it was accepted. I was glad to find something else to do that would still involve writing but that wasn't writing a novel. I had grown up knowing about black writers at home—Sterling Brown and my grandmother were first cousins—but black literature was not something I had studied in college. Writing book reviews became a way for me to read black writers again.

A lot of what we take for granted now was not available in the late seventies. Many of the African-Americans who are writing literary criticism now were not around then. Which made it both a difficult time and also an amazing time to be a writer. It was a period of real discovery. Maybe everyone feels this way about his or her apprenticeship. Maybe some of us ought to never consider our apprenticeships as being over. What I liked about writing reviews is that something that I had written would appear, my friends would ring me up and we would talk about it, and then after a week or two the review would disappear and not be a bother anymore. It was a form of exhibitionism, and yet it maintained some sort of anonymity. I could have my say, but there wasn't a long-lasting paper trail back to me.

Review writing also allowed me a certain amount of marginality. I didn't really have to take into account various calculations about what was going on outside of critical judgment. When I was writing reviews, I felt as though nothing was riding on them, and so I was free to make them the best I could. I was free to put everything I wanted or didn't want into it because it wasn't part of my résumé or my curriculum vitae; it was just about the book I was reviewing.

It is hard to remember exactly when I started writing *High Cotton* because bits and pieces of it were in a drawer for a very long time—writing that I wasn't sure would work, chunks that I felt might work but didn't know where or how. To support myself while I was writing, I worked as a secretary sometimes at *The New York Review of Books*. I started writing for *The Review* long before I worked there. You could say that I grew up there. And then I left the country because I needed to be someplace else. I moved to Berlin, where a whole separate and colorful life opened up for me. Robert Wilson asked me to work in the theater, which meant collaborating with an East German playwright named Heiner Muller, a very intriguing character. I wrote "texts" for what were not plays but rather *theater*. In Wilson's vision, everything depends on everything else—the lights, makeup, set, props, choreography, and the text all carry equal weight. It was interesting, and also sitting in on rehearsals all day you make friends, and so I was able to skip that lonely time of being in a new town and not knowing anyone.

I chose Berlin because, before the Wall came down, Berlin was a very poor city—a forgotten city, a completely subsidized city. The only business in Berlin was culture. There were no businessmen, there were no politicians. So the students and the intellectuals there had an exaggerated prominence. It seemed to me like an unending festival of symphonies, paintings, readings, and nightclubs where everyone wore black.

During the time when I lived in Berlin, any kind of German nationalism was something that we ridiculed because we considered it to be obsolete; it had been *that* generation that did *that*. It was that type of thing where the young, beatnik generation ran the show, which made racism toward me as a black American a nonissue. (Berlin was also, technically, an occupied city at that time, so there was no sense of intimidation as an American.)

My reason for leaving the States was not so much because I didn't like it here, but because I think that New York in particular changed in the eighties. I shouldn't lump the eighties into one generalization because then I'm doing what Susan Sontag calls "false decade thinking"—the sixties are this, the seventies are that, the eighties are this, and so on. In reality our history is much more confused. Nevertheless, the people who made New York what it was in my mind were not moving to New York anymore because of the increased cost of living. Big money took over cultural institutions, and everything started to look very different to me; the ballet became high profile, big businesses bought small, independent art magazines, publishing houses became part of large conglomerates. Suddenly there were people living in New York who had no connection whatsoever with that cultural tradition of cosmopolitan migration, and neoconservatism began a constant attack on liberal cultural. That drove me crazy. There was this surge of ambition that had a very dishonest air about it. And it happened among blacks too. To this day, I don't recognize or relate to New York the way I once did.

You don't notice the distance of living abroad until you can't follow a news story back home. I wasn't in the States during the Anita Hill hearings, and so the news that I received abroad was very dramatic, but the thing that shocked me the most was that every black person who testified was Republican. I suppose it should not have shocked me so much, since we'd had a Republican administration for ten years, and the only way black people in politics could get a job was by being Republican. Still, it was all very shattering to me. What broke my heart about Clarence Thomas's nomination was that it demonstrated Bush's contempt for the Supreme Court and his contempt for black people. And that there were actually black people who were saying, "Well, you have to go along with him [Clarence Thomas] because he is black." It shows how much we have lost morally and ethically. Thurgood Marshall didn't stand only for being black, he stood for excellence.

In terms of black men in this country, everyone is talking about our "plight," but nobody really knows what the "plight" is, though there is no shortage of writing on the subject. I read a statistic that fifty-seven percent of black men in Baltimore are either in jail, on parole, or have a warrant out against them. The newspapers report daily on what the black man's prospects are: he can either work at McDonald's for nonunion wages, or he can work for a little while selling drugs and make a lot of money. That is the expectation for the black man—that his choices are limited. But the condition precedes the expectation.

We have also come back to a place where the street and the black vernacular signify authentic blackness, and where everything other than that is either Eurocentric or Uncle Tommin'. There are black people everywhere in various social and professional settings who will put on their "street style" to save face because it has the prestige and is the blackest of black. I don't believe this to be true. W.E.B. Du Bois wasn't very street, and yet his blackness was authentic.

It used to be that when writers like Leroi Jones would make oppositions in his poetry about "soul brother" versus "uptight black bourgeois," it was really an attack on American materialism. Criticism of the American system was implicit in black literature. Not just criticism of racism or of Jim Crow, but of the society where these things were possible. There is less of this kind of criticism now in part because we have a larger black middle class. We're all economic hostages, hostages to the sanctity of the free market and private enterprise. The collapse of our critical edge has left no philosophical alternative, and we are now suffering from collapse of social will and ineffective central government. Somehow we have lost the willingness to apprehend a true picture of our society.

It is hard to say what authentic blackness is. There are so many ways of looking at black. For instance, jazz music is authentically black, but it is also authentically American. I remember seeing a talk show, "Oprah," or something like that, and it featured white hip-hop kids whose parents were either upset or not upset. The show also featured the black response to these kids, which was generally very angry. It was strange because I didn't see any reason why those kids shouldn't be interested in black styles and black trends—why not? This is what black people have been asking for—that our culture be moved to the center. But when this happens, everyone gets upset and cries exploitation, or loss of purity. I mean, you can hate Vanilla Ice with good reason, but otherwise we might do well to champion the infiltration of black culture into the American mainstream.

Furthermore on the notion of black authenticity—it is not just cultural, but it is also historical; we have shared an emotionally trying historical experience. And we are not alone in that. Blackness can also be socially defined, meaning that it can change from moment to moment. It can be defined psychologically—whether it is pride or self-hatred. I think blackness is a combination of all of these definitions.

The reason I keep writing is because I can't do anything else, not because I enjoy it. Well, I guess I do enjoy the physical act of writing, as long as it's not the first draft.

The wire mesh of our screen porch was as black as Ray Charles's sunglasses. I could watch the world go by, but the known world could not see me in my robes of state, scepter and orb in hand. I appeared in full regalia on the ramparts of the Tower only when my parents and sisters were not at home and the sitter was on the telephone, at which time two burgundy comforters became available, as well as a cummerbund, assorted buttons and brooches, a black lacquer cane that a bridge player had forgotten and would never find again, and a puffy black velvet hat from that region of the upstairs hall closet where my mother consigned clothing she would no longer be caught dead in.

The steep hill of our yard became the cliffs of Dover. The street, Capitol Avenue, which I was forbidden to step into under pain of never being allowed outside again, sleepy Capitol Avenue with its regulation elms, was the English Channel. Classmates who threw rocks from their doors across the street lived in France. The school crossing up the sidewalk was Hadrian's Wall. Then came Scotland and, farther north, the terra incognita of houses with driveways. The corner filling station down the sidewalk I cast as the Atlantic. There the game ended. Beyond the filling station were many bad corners, crumbling limestone bridges, and the serious business of "downtown."

The role of traitor went to Buzzy. His crimes included calling me a liar when I said I saw the Beatles at the state fair and saying that the Beatles said they would never let a nigger like me kiss their boots. Buzzy was a certifiable hoodlum: he wore sleek Stacy Adams shoes without socks. It was only a matter of time before he had his hair konked and rolled up in one of those damp scarves favored by thugs on bad corners. On a field trip to Monticello he managed to get the class so worked up that people at rest stops asked our shame-faced chaperones if we were orphans.

Buzzy lived on Hadrian's Wall, on the corner above the school crossing, in a house that was half painted and almost as dilapidated as our wrecked boat. Buzzy's hill had mange. A Ford had averted another Ford and careened almost up to his porch. The grass wouldn't grow back. He often stayed home to take care of his mother, a woman whose hair had a *National Geographic* wildness.

He was allowed to stay up and drink 7-Up when his mother had company. She sometimes went through party moods. Cars parked all the way down to our house. The whole block tried not to hear the music. Buzzy wasn't sent to bed when the adults began to talk like adults. His mother's friends didn't coo, pinch his cheeks, and wait for him to go upstairs in pajamas he was too old for. They came in shooting from the hip, as I saw it. He'd already tasted beer.

He was twelve, a bulldog with fists like the muscle men's in the back-page ads of comics. His osprey eyes gave him a clean shot at prey tromping home with pressed maple leaves, paper Halloween pumpkins, irregular Christmas stars, and Easter baskets caked with Elmer's glue. The safety patrol was too scared to blow the whistle on him. The white principal agreed with parents that Buzzy was a candidate for reform school, until Buzzy's mother flew out of her *National Geographic* remoteness and made a scene in his office and all over the hall, after which the principal took the line that no Negro boy was too young to learn to defend himself.

Buzzy made being good look like a sort of fatalism. At most, "behaving" meant that you were sometimes left alone, left to make what you wanted of the *Illustrated London News*. Mostly, your waking hours were a tight schedule of obligations and activities to be gotten through quickly, like the magical checklist of your prayers. The teachers said Buzzy was being selfish when he disrupted class. But he wasn't. He was sacrificing himself. He was the Dessalines of the fourth grade, the deep seeker who, wanting things to be different, could only hammer away at the way things were.

Buzzy had positioned himself on our steps. "That's my car," he promised himself when one he liked went by. He was known to drop stolen baseball bats or to let go of my neck to stand in rapture as a Stingray roared by carrying a demon who held the thread of life in his hands. Traffic had a sedative effect on Buzzy, like a fire or a tank of fish.

Cars were sacred anyway in Indianapolis, the "All-American City." The miracle of speed brought out the pioneer fervor. The new dealerships behind the state house and the used lots on the fringes of the airport, decorated with placards, chattering flags, and strings of dancing bulbs, possessed the healing power of revivalist sects. Come forward, brethren, and accept this Coupe de Ville. The Memorial Day race—"White Trash Day," Grandfather called it—was a tradition of beer cans thrown from passing cars, white Pat Boone shoes, checkered trousers, white belts, increased highway fatalities, and condoms peeking up in the reservoirs like water moccasins. Buzzy was at his least belligerent when one of his mother's friends said he'd take him to the Speedway for the time trials.

Sweat weakened the brim of my crown and smudged my lenses as the traitor studied the English Channel and crushed a praying mantis between his fingers. I would have mounted an honorable attack with my cane had the shushing of my robes not given me away. I stood under the August sun covered in bedspreads and ornamented like a Christmas tree.

"Make me faint," Buzzy said.

He was careful with me ever since my sisters had sold their

stock of car brochures to him. He'd gone into his mother's purse while she slept it off on top of her stereo cabinet with the bass thumping through her. But I thought my appearance provocative enough for Buzzy to send my scepter like a javelin through one of the pinned-together curtains of our hermit neighbor, the Last of the Mohicans. He showed so little interest in the chance to pick on me that I decided he was sick.

A Rolls, the first ever sighted on Capitol Avenue, purred down the street. I jumped out of my garb. "Don't act like you never had nothing," Buzzy said. I put my hand in my pocket too late. The old woman in the back seat must have seen me wave to her chrome. I told Buzzy that the tangerine hidden in my hat had come all the way from California.

"Them niggers out in California crazy. My daddy saw them."

I tried not to interrupt, but it irritated me when Buzzy got out of his depth. Wat Tyler led the Peasant Rebellion, I had to tell him, way back in history. They burned manor houses and tax collectors, but that was in my England.

"Is not. Watts in California," Buzzy insisted. I gave up, collected the symbols of my authority, and withdrew.

Unless my parents admitted that Wat Tyler's riot happened in 1381 and the Magna Carta in 1215, I was going to stuff my ears with Brussels sprouts. I was given the opportunity to reconsider my tone in my room, where I sat folding my collars under to make my jackets like the Beatles'.

I heard the whole neighborhood at play in the diffuse after-dinner light. My sisters had invented a new game for my friends, a combination of Go Fish and Bread and Butter Come and Get Your Supper. They christened it Call Out the National Guard. Buzzy used the switch on stragglers and screamed, "Kill, kill, kill, burn, burn, burn," with such realism that my parents sent him home.

ISHMAEL REED

ISHMAEL REED is the author of more than twenty books, which include novels, essays, plays, and poetry. He has been a finalist for the Pulitzer Prize and was twice nominated for the National Book Award. Reed has been a lecturer at the University of California at Berkeley for twenty years. He is the founder of the Before Columbus Foundation and a member of the PEN Oakland group and the American Council for the Arts. His best-known works include the satirical and influential novels *Yellow Back Radio Broke-Down* (1969) and *Reckless Eyeballing* (1970). Reed's most recent works are *Japanese by Spring* (1993) and a collection of essays written in his trademark iconoclastic and probing style called *Airing Dirty Laundry* (1994). He lives with his family in Oakland, California.

THE MAIN THING ABOUT MY WRITING is that it is not like any other. I have always strived to be original.

I was writing in a satirical style before it was even a style to be considered. It was not something that I thought out. I have always been suspicious of pomposity, arrogance, and hubris and have used many different writing techniques aside from satire to address that suspicion. I come from a working-class family, and we always ridiculed people who put on airs. My family never beat around the bush, we always spoke our minds and didn't take any bullshit. I'm the only member of my family who isn't armed, literally. I suppose my weapon is writing. So in part my background and upbringing led me to my style of writing. I also found that the standard, conventional literature I read was something that I knew that I would never write. My writing is real cutup, it's very provocative, and I make no apologies about that.

I had my writing style before I even started writing. The combination of a particular outlook that I had on the world and my own authentic personality dicatated the way I would proceed as a writer early on. Of course, many writers would say that style takes decades to master, which is true for some writers, but I am satisfied with the way that I have approached writing from the beginning—and that is to try and put a different angle on things, and to question the status quo. Writing is a lifetime occupation; I never know how or where I am going to end up, but I keep producing, and keep working at it.

The fact that all of my books are still in print is a constant source of reaffirmation. Books that I have written in 1969 are still in print—people still make references to their titles and their plots, and I still receive letters from people around the world telling me that they enjoy my work. Recently I did a reading in Korea from my latest book, *Japanese by Spring*, which is a pivitol work in terms of the changes I have made in my writing and the direction that I am beginning to move toward. I am very interested in introducing the African-American literary style to Asia in the same way that James Baldwin introduced the African-American novel to Europe. I chose Asia because I feel that in Asia there has not been much exposure to novels that are stylistically African-American.

I think I started off writing in a self-conscious, experimental kind of way. *Yellow Back Radio Broke-Down*, *Free-lance Pallbearers*, and *Mumbo Jumbo* were all part of that early period of writing for me. When I wrote *The Last Days of Louisiana Red*, I was beginning to make a transition in the work, and by the time I got to *Flight to Canada*, my writing had become more communicative to the average reader, and much less exclusive. *Japanese by Spring* is important because of the large audience that it reaches. My goal is to become a world-class writer, where I have constituencies in many different countries, and where I am not subject to the literary and cultural whims that the American marketplace imposes on black writers.

I have always maintained that writing is an art that gives me great pleasure, so I didn't choose writing simply because of the power I knew that it could wield. But it is true that I have chosen writing primarily because I feel that it is a medium that is able to compete more immediately and effectively in the marketplace of ideas. Consider how different it would be if Martin Luther King, Jr., had delivered his "March on Washington" speech on a saxophone, rather than delivering it by means of written and verbal articulation—writing can directly influence cultural, political, and sociological change. I use that analogy because Americans are often more comfortable with black people as musicians and athletes than they are with black people as writers, because writing is more subversive.

I am never concerned about losing audiences or constituencies when I take a stand. Many people are upset with what I have written about the feminist movement, which is a white, middle-class, self-indulgent movement that may include a few black divas but that functions primarily as a distraction to more pressing issues. I am not the only person who holds this opinion, yet my political position is singled out and continues to be distorted. I am suspicious of all -*isms*, and I have never joined a movement. To subscribe to an -*ism* implies that you are locked into one particular way of thinking, which is far too limiting for me. It is always important to remain open to facts, ideas, and other perspectives. I don't know what a pragmatist is—I consider myself an independent radical.

An example of the way that my political perspective has been distorted can be seen in the ongoing and often antagonistic relationship between me and the editors at *Ms.* magazine, which has been consistently twisted by people in the media. I had an exchange with Robin Morgan when she was the editor at *Ms.*, and I told her that it was hypocritical for her to jump on me when her magazine reflects the old plantation paradigm—white women running things, with black and Third World women in all of the slave quarter positions (contributing editor-ships, and what have you). *Ms.* magazine is a coorporate business, and when it changed format, and I read in *The New York Times* business section that *Ms.* was going to try to get the minority market—what that meant to me was that they were getting ready to hit on black men, because bashing black men is a sellable product. Sure enough, that is what the magazine did. Once the magazine became nonprofit, black men were attacked in every issue. My main concern with the editorial staff at *Ms.* magazine is their treatment of black people, particularly of black men.

We live in a time of slander, so if you are open to the public eye, you can expect to have something slanderous said about you. The worst accusation that could ever be made to me as a black man in America is that we are all the same. It is tremendously dangerous to lump black men all together in one category, or to blame one or all of us for the actions of one or a few black men. That makes me angry, and sometimes I am writing from that place of anger, and other times I am not. There is a whole range of emotions in my work, but I am definitely not afraid to be angry, which is an affront to some people. Black men have been through a lot of struggle, and we are expected to recover and to modify our behavior overnight. While that compromise may be the way to get over, I'm not going out like that. Black men pay for disinformation. We are marked by every bit of information that is untrue or heresay.

Oftentimes white critics get so threatened by black male writers that they can't praise one without signifying on the others. This happens with black women writers as well. For example, the reintroduction of Ralph Ellison into the mainstream after all of this time (referring to the March 14, 1994, *New Yorker* interview) was a direct response to Toni Morrison winning the Nobel Prize. The white media needed to bring back to the forefront this man who was near death and who wrote an important novel many years ago as a way of diminishing the stature of Toni Morrison's achievement as a Nobel Prize Laureate.

The same thing happened when Amiri Baraka first became controversial—then the media also brought up Ralph Ellison. Every time a black writer gains any kind of prominence, particularly of the revolutionary, social, and cultural perspective changing sort, the media brings up Ralph Ellison, whose novel, *Invisible Man*, ends with the first person taking no position—or rather dropping out with a long anti-Stalinist speech. Moreover, *The New Yorker* is a white separatist publication, which makes me suspicious of its praising the universality of black writers. You seldom see a poem or a fiction excerpt by a black writer in *The New Yorker*. They may have a guest native writer one day, but that's about it. The magazine always has a token, but it is fundamentally a separatist publication run by whites, where the stories are written by and about white people, and the seldom-seen black writers are brought in for comic relief.

Not everyone is going to pick up an issue of *The New Yorker* and immediately think that it is a white separatist publication, and I have admittedly pursued a thorough analysis of the publication that most people wouldn't bother spending the time on. However, since I have spent the time, I know what's up with the magazine, and I don't mind making a sophisticated analysis of my findings for the general public. If *The New Yorker* believes in the universality of Ralph Ellison, then why doesn't *The New Yorker* hire some black people? Sure, I've seen Henry Louis Gates's articles in there—sometimes he writes the whole issue of *The New York Times*—but I'd like to see him share some of his power. When it comes to *The New Yorker* and other publications that he writes for—where white scholars can get published with the snap of a finger—unless it's Cornel West, Gates is the token black scholar or writer. Henry Gates and Cornel West are not the only smart black people in this country. There are black people on my block who are smart. But the media picks out one or two black people to deify, and he or she who is picked tends to get comfortable in his or her position.

There are many battles to choose from, but right now I am focused on the media. The media influences public perception, and what is happening now is that it has become extremely segregated, where we have whites discussing black issues. All we see is this sort of hocus pocus view of African-American reality, while African-Americans have no way of combating that falsehood. I'm part of a group called PEN Oakland, in which I have organized a campaign against the media. My ultimate hope with the campaign is that we will be able to develop a more multicultural network where colored and white ethnics would share airtime. What we have now is a media that is run by a small group of white men who require that any people of color who work for them must submit to their point of view. I don't expect that the people of color who have chosen to make that submission will necessarily want to give up their slots, but I do feel that they will get tired of seeings things played out the way they are and could only feel relief at the group's attempts to set the system fair and square.

I think that affirmative action has done very well for white women. After a recent bogus symposium in New York on black-Jewish relations, Michael Lerner wrote in *Time* magazine that Jewish women have benefitted the most from affirmative action. Then Paul Berman wrote in *The New Yorker* that Jewish people are upset about black people receiving affirmative action. Lerner is, of course, right. The level of debate on that issue is that absurd. So no, I don't believe affirmative action has helped African-Americans all that much.

Everybody is always talking about how black people need to change, but white people are the ones who need to change. Whenever I say that other people need to change, I get these neo-conservative, wisecracking responses from the major publications. The white people who own this country have a settler mentality, and they are always afraid of a black uprising. That's why folks are jumping all over rap music right now—critics have lost their minds over rap music, talking about the bad behavior of rap artists—folks are afraid of the rise of these rappers, yet Grace Slick of the Jefferson Airplane held off some cops with a twelve-gauge shotgun??? I would like to see some of these rappers, and other entertainers in advantageous positions, use their power more effectively. Someone like Mike Tyson, who is an intellectual with a brilliant mind, could inspire a lot of kids to pursue intelligent avenues. I get frustrated when I see people like Tyson and some of these rappers who have all of that money and who are often very smart not using their means to that end.

I enjoy being an African-American, and I feel that there is a joy in black culture that is very unique. And yes, very marketable. It is no wonder that some white people are fascinated by us—we have fun, are more relaxed, and have a stronger sense of livelihood. As long as we are choosing our markets, putting the money in our own accounts, and spending the money on our own terms, okay. Otherwise, we need to question it.

I never feel lonely inside of my convictions about society, and there isn't much that I fear. The one concern I have is the same as any other black man in America—that I will walk out the door and become a casualty. It's not that I feel that the society is conspiratorial, I just call it like I see it. And if I weren't writing, I'd be throwing bricks.

From
YELLOW BACK RADIO
BROKE-DOWN

If it isn't the alienated individualist stuck out here in the desert, the leader of these grim horsemen said.

It was Bo Shmo and the neo-social realist gang. They rode to this spot from their hideout in the hills. Bo Shmo leaned in his saddle and scowled at Loop, whom he considered a deliberate attempt to be obscure. A buffoon an outsider and frequenter of sideshows.

Bo Shmo was dynamic and charismatic as they say. He made a big reputation in the thirties, not having much originality, by learning to play Hoagland Howard Carmichael's "Buttermilk Sky" backwards. He banged the piano and even introduced some novel variations such as sliding his rump across the black and whites for that certain affect.

People went for it. It was in all the newspapers. He traveled from coast to coast exhibiting his ass and everything was fine until the real Hoagland Howard Carmichael (the real one) showed up and went for Bo Shmo's goat. He called him a lowdown patent thief and railed him out of town. You would think that finding themselves duped, the imposter's fans would demand his hide. Not so, Americans love being conned if you can do it in a style that is both grand and entertaining. Consider P. T. Barnum's success, Semple McPherson and other notables. A guy who rigs aluminum prices can get himself introduced by Georgie Jessel at 100 dollars a plate but stealing a can of beer can get you iced.

■

So sympathetic Americans sent funds to Bo Shmo which he used to build one huge neo-social realist Institution in the Mountains. Wagon trains of neo-social realist composers writers and painters could be seen winding up its path.

Hey Bo, one of his sidekicks spoke up. We'd better blast this guy right off the way I look at it. Nobody will miss him since he went out with that carnival. If he makes it across the desert he might land a typewriter and do a book on his trials. He'll corner the misery market and pound out one of those Christian confessionals to which we are so much endeared. Then where will we be. How will we buy all these campy cowboy suits . . .

Shut up, Bo said slapping the man in the face with his prospector's cap. The other horsemen remained mute. Bo Shmo did all their thinking for them. Their job was merely to fold their arms and look mean at the hoedowns or rather the shakedowns. You see Bo Shmo was a real collectivist. Worked hard at it. Fifty toothbrushes cluttered his bathroom and when he walked down the street it seemed a dozen centipedes headed your way. He woke up in the morning with crowds and went to bed with a mob. The man loved company. It seemed that he wore people under his coat although none of them would pull it for him. He resembled Harpo Marx at times, you know, the scene where Harpo has shoplifted a market and stuffed all the smoked hams under an oversized coat. He looked like that.

The trouble with you Loop is that you're too abstract, the part time autocrat monarchist and guru finally said. Crazy dada nigger that's what you are. You are given to fantasy and are off in matters of detail. Far out esoteric bullshit is where you're at. Why in those suffering books that I write about my old neighborhood and how hard it was every gumdrop machine is in place while your work is a blur and a doodle. I'll bet you can't create the difference between a German and a redskin.

What's your beef with me Bo Shmo, what if I write circuses? No one says a novel has to be one thing. It can be anything it wants to be, a vaudeville show, the six o'clock news, the mumblings of wild men saddled by demons.

All art must be for the end of liberating the masses. A landscape is only good when it shows the oppressor hanging from a tree.

Right on! Right on, Bo, the henchmen chorused.

Did you receive that in a vision or was it revealed to you?

Look out now Loop don't get quippy with me, I'll have one of my men take you off. We can't afford the luxury of individualism gumming up our rustling. We blast those who don't agree with us.

Aw leave me alone Bo Shmo to doing my thing which for now is dying. You presume to be able to give other people decrees—living in your expensive neo-social realist retreat while commonfolk who follow your rants try to match their nickel plates with aeroplanes and tanks. One of these days those people are going to rise up from the pavement where they died clutching coupons and unredeemable refuse from shop windows and take it out on your hide.

■

O.K. fat mouth, you asked for it. Discipline him fellows. The horsemen dismounted and began to put Loop through changes. Being neo-social realist and not very original they gave him a version of Arab Death. They smeared jelly on his face and buried him up to the neck in desert. Soon his face would be crawling with vermin which was certainly no picnic of a way to go.

Suddenly above them a whirring noise.

Gads! Bo said, the arch-nemesis of villains like me. The Flying Brush Beeve Monster. Let's get out of here.

The horsemen mounted their nags and with Bo Shmo out front headed back to their institution in the mountains.

Not only would he be a desert carrion, but now something right out of Science Fiction was descending upon him from the heavens, Loop thought. It resembled a monster insect whatever it was and when it landed it stirred up the sand so that Loop couldn't make out its dimensions. Much to his surprise a plainclothes Indian casually stepped out of the monster's belly. He held a cigarette holder in his hand. He strode to the position where Loop'd been tied down in the sand and lifted a canteen to the outlaw's lips.

Champagne! Who are you?

Never mind my man, I was on the way to Europe for an appointment with my tailor when I happened upon you surrounded by those mediocre bandits. The desert was fine until they moved into those hills coming out of their fancy hideout only to make raids on sniveling and s/m liberals that take that sick tour.

What tour?

O there's this Royal Flush Gooseman, a rattlesnake heart if there ever was, he hires wagon trains which bring liberals out here for the purpose of having the trains surrounded by Bo Shmo and his henchmen. The whole thing is staged if you ask me. Since my people are no longer around to raise war parties Bo Shmo and his men are taking all the loot. Deserts are for visions not for materialists. Read any American narrative about crossing—apparitions, ravens walking about as tall as men, the whole golden phantasmagoria. Maybe I can give you a lift to Video Junction, the town lying about 50 miles from here?

Loop regarded the Monster with apprehension.

O don't worry about that. I created it to get around in, made it from spare parts I found in deserted ghost towns. I also used a new kind of plant called plastic I discovered growing in the hills like wildfire.

I'm a kind of patarealist Indian going about inventing do dads. This machine comes in better than nags and creaky stagecoaches. Stupid shmucks and boobs around here think it's some kind of flying ghost cow. Legends, whispering among the peasants, protective charms on the door of each house. The whole bit. Bo Shmo and the cattlemen are in the same routine. Afraid of anything that can get off the ground, materialists that they are—anything capable of groovy up up and aways strikes terror in their hearts.

■

The Indian freed Loop and escorted him to his hobby lying in the sand.

I call it a helicopter, lots of mileage on very little fuel, but I wouldn't be surprised if bad medicine steals the patents and calls them his own. Honkie. Devil.

Loop smiled.

John D. Rockefeller didn't have an original idea in his life and George Gershwin stole pillows from sleeping Negroes plush vampire that he was and where did you think Mae West got her manic depressive female swishing? In New York City as you read me now some woman done took Martha and the Vandellas "Dancing In The Streets" and calls it her very own.

You listen to Soul Music, Chief?

Sure man; all the time, the Indian replied releasing the wheel of the helicopter and breaking into a strong boogaloo from the waist up. The craft rocked.

I don't even want to go into how Moses sneaked around the Pharaoh's court abusing this hospitality by swiping all the magic he could get his clutches around. If I run down that shit, Loop, the book won't be reviewed in Manhattan . . . and look what the Fiend did to us. We showed the cat how to ride, what to wear, how to plant, woodcraft, how to tan, tried to teach them riding bareback but they were so repressed they had to use a saddle, and on Friday nights we introduced a new recreation for these dull creatures.

GREG

TATE

G REG TATE is a senior staff writer for the New York–based paper the *Village Voice*. His essays on contemporary culture have been published in *The New York Times*, *Vibe* magazine, *The Washington Post*, *Rolling Stone*, *Premiere* magazine, and *L.A. Weekly*. A collection of his essays, *Flyboy in the Buttermilk* (1992), is now in its fourth printing. Tate is also involved in theater, and his play *My Darlin' Gremlin*, a collaboration with composer Butch Morris, premiered in June 1993 at City College of New York's Aaron Davis Hall as part of the New Voices/New Visions series. A working musician, Tate leads the funkadelic band Women in Love. The group's debut CD and songbook were released in September 1994 on the band's own Mrs. Jones label. Tate currently lives in Harlem and is working on his first novel.

I WAS REALLY INTO COMIC BOOKS as a kid and had begun writing and drawing my own comics when I decided to write one about a trumpet player in the twenty-first century. I went down to the Dayton public library and got a whole bunch of books on music. One of the books I got out was Leroi Jones's *Black Music*. The quality of his writing made me intrigued with music, but it also encouraged me to read more of his work—his poetry and short shories—which led me to the works of other black writers, poets, and fiction writers.

When I started writing I wanted to do a couple of things. I loved, and was inspired by, the bizzare imagery in Leroi Jones's (alias Amiri Baraka) poetry. I was fascinated by the way he would juxtapose things that were romantic with things that were horrific. He has one line in a poem about gangrenous Tootsie Rolls. I was also very interested in music at that time, and I would have metaphorical flashes, insights, or visions from listening to music. I began looking for ways to trans*literate* what I was feeling and receiving from music into writing.

When I began to write music criticism much later on, postcollege, I was attempting to write music reviews as sort of poetic essays. My interest in writing, especially when I first started writing, was mainly to see how wild I could make the writing while still keeping it somewhat contained. I wasn't even all that concerned if any of it made sense. Some of the early pieces that I wrote were like long prose poems that would eventually find their way around to talking about whatever musical artist I was meant to be reviewing. In a lot of ways, music represents to me the highest form of artistic freedom and a great liberation in terms of expressivity. Especially black *expressivity*. Particularly in the kinds of music that I've been drawn to—George Clinton, and then all of the so-called avant-garde jazz artists from the fifties and sixties—because it seemed as though that type of music came from a time when there were no walls, no limits, and no boundaries to what could be done. That same spirit has definitely infused into my writing.

Both music and writing came into light for me at the same time, and each is a very important part of my life; I just get paid more to write. It's been really interesting trying to juggle the band with writing. I'm in a very fortunate position here at the *Village Voice*, where the nature of the paper is such that it really looks after its writers, particularly writers who have become identified with it over time. The editors here give me a lot of space to do what I have to do both contractually and spiritually.

It's kind of strange the way I started writing professionally. I had been writing music reviews for local papers in Washington, D.C., for about three or four years when a friend of mine who had moved from D.C. to New York started writing for the *Voice*. She kept telling me to send some of my writing to the music editor. I finally sent him something, and I will always remember what he said: "I can't use this piece, but the more writing I get like this, the better the chances are that I will want to use it in the future." It was a big ego boost to be living in Washington and writing for a New York paper. It was a thrill, almost like some sort of escape. I had always known that writing was going to be a part of my life, but it had not occurred to me to identify it as a profession.

A couple of months after I started writing for the *Voice*, I got a call from this woman in New York named Linda Bryant, who ran an art gallery called Just Above Midtown. She wanted to put together a black arts festival and needed a music curator. Somebody who had read my reviews in the *Voice* had turned her on to me, and she called to ask me if I would come up to New York for a meeting. So I went, and after that meeting, a series of strange and fortuitous events followed in sequence. I stayed for the meeting, which lasted a week, and then my editor at the *Voice* told me that he was going on vacation for three weeks and that I was welcome to stay in his house in the Village while he was gone. To make a long story short, I fell in love in New York, went back to D.C., packed up my stuff, and that was it! I thought, just do the lean times, you know, roll and tumble with the times, do whatever I got to do to survive. And I guess it all worked out in the end.

The surprising thing was that I didn't know until I came up to New York that people had actually been following my writing— that it had actually meant something to people, especially because I had only been doing it for such a short time. I remember going to the Ritz after I'd been up here for a minute, and the doorman said, "You Greg Tate?" I said yes, and he said, "I always wondered what you looked like." It was weird that people were interested in who I was. When I was in D.C., I knew that my brother read my stuff, you know, a couple of other people read the *Voice* articles, and I figured that that was the extent of it. Which was cool, I was happy just to be in print. But I soon learned that there were other editors who were following my writing, and that it was possible for me to generate more work.

I think the high point of writing for me during that early pe-riod was being commissioned by *Down Beat* magazine to write this two-part series on Miles Davis. His music, and the era from which it came, was really important to me, and I felt that it had been misunderstood by everyone else who had written about it up to that point. So it was like a great act of revenge to actually be able to write that piece in *Down Beat*. It was an instance when my writing just flowed. There were things in that piece that I had been wanting to say for so long that when I was given the opportunity, it all just came in one fell swoop. I remember it was like writing in some kind of fever dream or something. I think I wrote the whole thing in two or three days straight.

I do tend to get transported in my writing, and very isolated. There are also definitely times when I feel like I'm having private arguments with people. Certain moments after I have finished a sentence feel like scoring a point, or like being in a boxing match and landing the knockout punch on somebody—like POW! Maybe that's the whole macho Hemingway element of writing. Toni Morrison talks a lot about the evasiveness of writing in her book *Playing in the Dark*. Every writer develops certain devices, and many that are used for masking emotions. I can be writing from a fever pitch of rage, but part of the way that I deal with that rage is by actually working it into the structure of the writing, so that the emotion becomes in many ways invisible.

Sometimes I will articulate something before I realize from what position I am speaking. But I understand as a black writer that I do have a responsibility to take a stand or to speak up for greater participation and for greater outreach to the black community, and other communities of color. For the most part, any sense of responsibility to black people that I may feel, particularly as a journalist, is something that I have inherited from my parents. My parents instilled this old kind of race-person sense of mission because they were both very active in the civil rights movement. When we lived in Ohio, they were part of this group of folks that ran an African-American cultural center. So when the Stokely Carmichaels and members of the Panthers would come to Dayton, these folks would come through our house. It was kind of like they were uncles or cousins or older brothers, they were just around. I remember staying at my grandmother's house, watching the

March on Washington on television, and knowing that my parents were there—it definitely shaped the nature of my encounters with race in this society for the rest of my life.

In terms of the kind of literature I am interested in, I have been forever drawn to the bizarre. I love science fiction novels because they offer a perspective that is different from the normal, mundane way of looking at the world. I am interested in people who manipulate distortions in the interest of design, to paraphrase Ralph Ellison. I am drawn to black writers who have occupied another space inside of our culture apart from what we normally associate with being black.

To a certain extent, writers are important to me because of the stands that they have taken up in the name of the race, but essentially, the act of taking a stand and getting out there is more significant to me than the stand itself. I read Ishmael Reed and argue with him. I read Amiri Baraka and argue with him. I read Skip Gates and argue with his stuff too. And then when I get a sense of who writers are, even if I just know a little bit about their personal lives, I take certain things with a grain of salt. I can tell where the chinks are, I understand where the writer is coming from, and I can see what their contradictions are. But my interest in a writer's personal life never goes beyond how it may relate to their writing.

I'm always surprised when people are interested in me as opposed to just what I write. I have never had any interest in writers as icons or idols. I never expect them to be the living embodiment of what they write. I like what certain writers do, but it would feel weird meeting a writer whose work I admire, in a contrived or planned sort of way. I just hear people. People seem to have this urge to know and divulge things they know about writers, which is very odd to me. I might like to meet Ralph Ellison at a bus station or something like that, totally accidentally. Maybe I wouldn't even recognize who he was, we'd just start talking.

When I was a kid, my parents brought me with them to this Black Power conference in Cleveland. During a break, I went into a local diner to get some boysenberry pie. The diner was full of middle-aged, elderly white folks, but there was this one older brother in there, probably in his midtwenties. He came over and started talking to me, and I didn't think much of it. We finished up eating around the same time and walked out of the diner together. Turns out we were both going back into the conference lobby, and once we got inside, homeboy wanted to start sparring with me. So he starts tagging me, but not hard enough to really hurt me, just so I'd feel it. Pretty soon a bunch of people started gathering around and everybody is watching me and this other brother with glee in their eyes. When my pop came over, I was expecting him to jump in between us, but he just watched with everybody else, like this is all cute and everything. Finally I realized that the person who was sparring with me was Muhammad Ali. That's the only way I would ever want to meet a writer whose work has influenced or inspired me.

I wouldn't deny that writing is an extension of the writer himself, but I think it's very different when people project these expectations on you because of what you write. Not expectations in terms of values, but when people become interested in who the writer is as a person in an almost gossip column kind of way, it doesn't feel right. I love talking about the things I'm interested in intellectually, creatively, and artistically, or about the structure of a novel and what makes it work. That kind of interest is cool, but the personal analysis of who a writer is is not so cool.

I'm interested in writers for writing and that's it. As an adolescent, I can remember wanting to read certain books because I knew that the writer was black, but ultimately it was the book that they had written that made the difference. When I discovered *The Bluest Eye* in my high school library—it slammed hard, hit me like a ton of bricks. The book has so much of a life of its own. I feel like I know more about Toni Morrison from reading that book than I could ever know, or want to know, from having a conversation with her, because there's so much in the story that is deeper than her. *The Bluest Eye* carries within its pages a whole place, time, and community of its own. I feel the same way when I sit down and read Amiri Baraka's writing because even though I know a lot about his background, I don't think about that, ain't even interested. It's definitely about—damn! Wish I could write a poem like that! Sometimes I walk around New York, and I will see or feel something that will make me think of a certain line from one of Baraka's poems. Baraka could be from a whole other century, or another country, all I need to know is that he is writing, and that I am affected by it. I'm not interested in what he's doing politically, or what he's going to say about Spike Lee making *Malcolm X*— that's not what drew me to the cat.

Right now I am working on a science fiction novel called *Alter'd Spayde*. In a broad sense, it's sort of like a progenitor to the black political methodology and the mythological figures of the sixties, except that it takes place in the next century. It concerns a friendship between two women—one is a deejay, and one a cultural anthropologist. The cultural anthropologist is the granddaughter of this figure whose name is Mandella Ain't Free, who led a mutant terrorist group in a race war that had been fought in the early part of the twenty-first century. Most of the story takes place in the present tense, but the anthropologist is researching her grandfather and the movement that he led, so there are also these documents from the period during which he was alive: manifestos, letters, and prose poems. A lot of what the sixties was about to me is the literature that it generated: documents, biographies, poetry. It becomes a running joke every time a new character is introduced in the story, because he or she always has some memoir, novel, or some biography that he or she starts reading or quoting from. All of these people have got their little books and what have you, which is a play on the slave net and how in the sixties everybody black and radical had a book out, and that's how the reader learns about the history and the world of the characters. It makes it fun to have this running gag and is also kind of interesting because the comic aspect can be used as one of the technical devices that holds the book together.

Skip Gates has talked about black novels as being revisions of other black novels. *Alter'd Spayde* is definitely my revision of maybe three different black novels: Ralph Ellison's *The Invisible Man*, Ishmael Reed's *Mumbo Jumbo*, and Toni Morrison's *Sula*. I remember reading an essay that Skip wrote about how the titles, as well as the stories, of black novels are also revisions—Richard Wright's *Native Son* beomes Ralph Ellison's *Invisible Man*, and such. I feel that *Alter'd Spayde* fits in there somewhere, and I finally feel as though I have arrived at this sense of ambitiousness about what I am doing as a writer.

In my mind, I am writing this book to go on a shelf next to those books I just mentioned. I want to make my novel as architectonic as *The Invisible Man*, where everything is symphonically interwoven, by detailing the depth of intimacy between the two women characters, down to their hair, their skin, the way certain things sound, and the way one person looks at the other. These are the types of things that give the whole writing process meaning. I know I'm writing this for eternity. I'm writing this for literary immortality. That's the objective. It's for other people to say if I get there or not. The novel is the last place where a writer can use all the resources of literature and writing: polemic, poetry, prose, the essay—all of these forms are at my disposal. It's a great kind of playground, or like an Erector set with words; I can feel myself building something. I get the Erector set, build it up, tear it down, make a big mess, and have fun with it. I'm definitely having fun working on this book.

I've been working on this novel off and on for about six years, but only in the last year have I felt as though I can really see the future through the eyes of the women in the story. At this point, I don't feel like I can make any wrong moves as far as their vision of what the future looks like and feels like. It's more the structural aspect of writing that continues to be an overriding concern, because it is difficult to maintain the discipline and the awareness of what makes a novel work. But the deeper I get into it, the more I feel like I know where I am, and where I'm going. Dizzy Gillespie said that when he and Charlie Parker played together, they weren't thinking about playing changes because at that point, the music was so much a part of their nervous system, they just played. Not to say that I'm at that level of talent, but I understand what Gillespie was talking about—when you get to a certain place technically, you don't really think about technique anymore, you just know it, you feel it. For me, having access to that place is what makes writing so joyful and pleasurable.

I could make up reasons for choosing black women as the central characters in my novel, and say we (black men) are supposed to love our sisters and you know, blah, blah, whatever, but the truth is that whenever I think about writing fiction, I am always immediately drawn to the powerful and symbiotic relationships among black women. The women who have made a difference in my life are women who have embraced their livelihoods, women who have dealt with and managed their fears. It's funny to hear the current debate or the assertions surrounding the "plight of the black man," because I just can't even hear that. It seems to me that much of this theory is an exploitation of the victim status. I can't even sit down and watch some of these films now about the pathetic black man—I can't even go there, because that's not how I see myself as a black man in this society.

I don't have a lot of patience when brothers start getting into this whole victim rap because in a lot of cases it seems that some of these brothers are trying to talk themselves into a cage. We all know what can happen out there; we all could go through the Rodney King thing—that could happen to any one of us, any given day of the week—but I don't live inside of that possibility as a political position. The issue has veered way off and now has absolutely nothing to do with really trying to address what it is that may be debilitating us in terms of our relationships with one another, with our children, and with those among us who are ill, have different styles or sexual preferences, or any of that.

Some racial obstacles are created in the mind. When we start talking about what we can and cannot do as black people, I think we have developed certain reflexes that are meant to dictate racist treatment. We're always trying to equalize the situation in our minds; to rationalize the inequity, or just turn it over. I was on my way somewhere the other day, and while I was standing there waiting for the bus, a cab pulled up and five white guys got into the cab. My reflex was: that cab driver would never let five brothers get in his cab. But then I thought: what are you talking about? You've been in a cab with five brothers before. It ain't going to be every cab driver, but there is a level of that victim mentality that we have programmed into ourselves, which leaves us always expecting inequity or unfairness to occur because we are black. We end up creating and fostering a certain kind of rage, which can cloud our clarity about what really needs to be focused on.

We can't address racism in society by critiquing minor racist acts of white individuals who we come across. We have to maintain some focus on the imbalance of power, and how the power is used. Racism is institutionally orchestrated in this society and always has been. People talk about institutional racism like it's something that we figured out, or that it became the target after the civil rights movement. Institutional racism was the target during slavery; slavery couldn't exist if it was legislated. That kind of systematic perspective on where the problem is and how to address it is what I see lacking in terms of the discussion around how black people need to move politically. And empathy is also lacking. In order to sit down and talk with any kind of black person, or white person, about the state of our racist society, we definitely need to stay open and allow ourselves to know that the lessons are going to come from everybody. And this falls in line with being a writer too—it's about maintaining, being able to release on our own egos enough to just let the lessons be taught.

I keep writing because of restlessness, bad nerves I guess. Writing is therapy for me. I consider writing to be one of the things that centers my life. I have a need to have things in my life that are private but that have the potential for some kind of larger relationship to other people. Through writing, I can verify my experience—the beginning and the receiving end of it. It has showed me degrees of great intuitive depth. I know that I have put some of my ideas together from outside information, and I could follow the information trail, but there are other ideas that I discover through writing that are incredible. And they're not just about relationships to other people, they're definitely about larger relationships . . . to the moon, the tides, and you know, mystery cycles.

From
MY DARLIN' GREMLIN
A PLAY

SEBASTIAN: As I've said before, it's not a religion. It's a spiritual and personal growth service for people who haven't learned how to properly honour the dead.

VERDREE: Not a religion? That's not what they say in the *Inquirer,* child. Is it true what they said about you and Demi Moore? I heard you had the child on her knees begging for mercy.

SEBASTIAN: You know me. Takin' no shorts and I pull more stunts than Bruce Willis. Bitch betta have had my money. But you know. I'm just doing what I have always done. Providing a service for those in need.

VERDREE: Yeah, yeah. I got your service angle, baby. And I know what you do for those in need. But, uh, run that part past me again about the impotent white boys . . .

SEBASTIAN: Infertility dear. This is white male infertility we're dealing with here. See, it's a well-known fact that white male fertility has fallen dramatically over the last two decades. The reason why is a less well-known but equally scientific fact.

After the travesties of Vietnam, white male souls stopped being reincarnated at the same rate as before. Consequently, white males not only can't reproduce in the same numbers as before, they can't even return from the well of souls in as large an amount either. As a consequence you have all these white male souls—

VERDREE: A contradiction in terms far as white boys go, but go on—

SEBASTIAN: All these white male souls wandering around the earth lost, getting into all types of mischief. You know how they do. So who you gonna call?

MISTER DANNY LOVE: Obviously not Ghostbusters.

SEBASTIAN: Look, you know white people do not know how to properly honor their ancestors. I chose to make this problem my problem because I was guided to do so while I was in a trance. An ancient African voice said unto me, help these lost white children get a grip on how to conduct themselves in the afterlife. Teach the living ones how to communicate with their ancestors and help put them to rest. So following that instruction, I arrange a kinship ritual between my clients and a surrogate white ancestor spirit. I also arrange for one of our more restless spirits of color to consider taking a lost white brother under their wing so to speak . . .

VERDREE: Hold up, wait a minute. Let me get this straight. You rope in some innocent black angel type sucker. Let's say he or she is just maxing and relaxing out there, cold chilling in the void. And you say, yo B, If you're free on Saturday, I need you to chauffeur a couple of savages over to a seance I'm doing for some of my Hollywood Euro trash—who, by the way, are paying yours truly, big bank, just for the experience. Damn Sebastian. Why you got to play our deceased brothers and sisters out like that. Bad enough we gotta be driving Miss Daisy down Sunset Boulevard. Must we drive trailor trash around the afterlife too? It all sounds like some New Age Aunt Jemima shit to me. I think your Aunt Truth is right. You going straight to hell, baby. Don't even think about them pearly gates.

SEBASTIAN: You know my motto. Service to the race for a profit.

VERDREE: I see your profits alright. But what race you talking about? And don't tell me the human race.

SEBASTIAN: Everything I do is guided by a higher source. It's a black thing you WOULDN'T understand.

VERDREE: Negress puh-leeze—I know you can do better than that . . .

SEBASTIAN: (*Turning on her fiercest West Indian patois.*) Woman listen. What being black means to you and what being black means to me are two different things. What it means to you is a bit of yesterday, edging up on today and suddenly staring down an unknown tomorrow. What it means to me encompasses all of eternity and the cosmos from the beginning of time. When they say to you, let's talk about being black in America you say, first we must talk about slavery and the Middle Passage. If someone asks me the same question, I say, first we must talk about the distribution ratio of hydrogen and helium molecules in the first hours of the universe's creation. Take into consideration how that initial explosion of energy accounts for all of life on earth today. Before we talk about being black in America we must go all the way back to the Big Bang. We must talk about black holes, white dwarfs, red giants, event horizons, and singularities. We must discuss chaos theory and the vibrational frequencies that keep nuclear elements from spinning apart. Stop me if I'm getting too deep for you, my sister.

VERDREE: (*Quoting liberally from George Clinton.*) Woman listen. You think you're saying something original here? You think I don't know we are just a biological speculation sitting here vibrating and we know not what we are vibrating upon? That the animal instinct in me tells me to live when I know it's time for me to die? Do y'all see my point?

JOHN EDGAR

WIDEMAN

JOHN EDGAR WIDEMAN received a degree in English from the University of Pennsylvania. Earning all-Ivy honors at Penn, he was awarded a Rhodes Scholarship to further his studies at the New School, Oxford University, England, where he earned a degree in philosophy. Wideman is the author of twelve books, including his widely praised nonfiction work *Brothers and Keepers* (1984), about his relationship with his imprisoned brother; *Fever* (1989), a collection of short stories; and his novel *Philadelphia Fire* (1990), based upon the 1985 bombing of Philadelphia's radical organization MOVE. Wideman, a two-time PEN/Faulkner Award winner, is a professor and associate dean of faculty at the University of Massachusetts at Amherst. *Fatheralong,* Wideman's autobiographical account of the history between himself and his father, was published in 1994. Wideman lives in Amherst with his wife and has three grown children.

THINK IT WAS NOT SO much a question of deciding that writing would be a way of thinking and of figuring things out for me, as it was a process of discovering that writing is what I could do.

Growing up in Pittsburgh, Pennsylvania, the public library was my tourist office. Not only for different places, but for different kinds of people, and different worlds. What was war like? What was it like to live in the Middle Ages? What was it like to be an Indian? I could do all of this mental voyaging through reading. When I began to think about writing, what I had learned from reading fertilized and organized the beginning of that process.

The more I read, the more I realized that writing was a kind of thinking that was different from any other kind of thinking. I had believed at one point that you first chose a subject, then worked at getting all of the necessary information about that subject, and only then could you write about it. But the more I read, the more I found out that writing starts with words. Those words create other words, and then those words create sentences, so that you are always making something. And that is thinking; starting with nothing, and ending with something.

There were a lot of things that I wanted to do, but I was born poor, so I also worried about stuff like eating, and having a roof over my head, and knowing where the next penny was coming from. I wanted to make sure that I had a day job. For me, it was always a sort of juggling act to take care of the necessities and be financially secure, and at the same time get away with doing exactly what I wanted to do. At one time, I thought I could manage that by being a professional athlete. That seemed to be a smart way to have a good life without working because if your work is something that you love, then you've beaten the system. After I got to college, it slowly became clear that no one was going to offer me the big bucks to play basketball. Then I started wondering what else I could do that wouldn't involve "working" but that would allow me to support myself.

I had thought that when I graduated from college I would like to pursue the possibility of playing in the Eastern Professional League, which was like a farm league for the NBA. I thought I would go to Princeton or some graduate school in the area so I could play for an Eastern League team. When the Rhodes Scholarship came along I had to make a real choice. I guess for the first time, I made an absolute decision that turned me to writing. That is to say, the reasons to go to Oxford were that it would give me a chance to see the world, and it would be a much less structured environment, and mainly I'd have time to write. Although choosing Oxford didn't necessarily promise any kind of job security or safety net, I decided that it was the right choice once I realized that I wanted to write more than anything else.

I never really left the world of my family, my brothers and sisters, and the realities of growing up black in America. There were times when I felt that I was on an extended vacation, and there were times when I felt AWOL, and there were confusions and conflicts and angers. My going away to college was a source of tension, a source of disequilibrium. On the other hand, I was able to go to places like the University of Pennsylvania and Oxford University, try things that I had never tried before, and deal with people who were totally different from me. I would never have been able to do any of that if I hadn't received a very powerful sense of identity and support from my family and my community. I brought with me to Oxford the strong preparation of a very wise and historically grounded community.

My family and I never had any arguments about what I was doing at school. Nobody at home had ever done the things that I was doing, so they couldn't be bossy or authoritative. They were spectators. They said, "If you're going to do it, just make sure you do your best. And be careful." And that was about it. What did they know about Oxford? And yet they knew *everything* about Oxford and how to help me with my experience there. Historically, we descend from people who were always on the edge, always in a kind of jeopardy, always required to do special things to survive. My family brought a kind of collective communal wisdom to me, and I was able to focus it on whatever I happened to be doing. Sometimes that cultural support was not consciously available to me. Only in retrospect do I see and understand how it helped me get through the toughest time. Often the strongest parts of your culture are the unconscious parts, the parts that you turn to by reflex.

Going on to teach at the college level was a very practical decison. I certainly could not have raised a family if I had considered myself a professional writer in the sense that I did nothing other than write. For me, professionalism has more to do with attitude than income. The people I consider to be my peers, the audience that I am writing for, and my willingness to expose writing of mine that I consider less than perfect, and then saying along with that, "This is the best I can do at this point, love it or leave it"—*that* is professionalism.

I'm also very ambitious. I think of writing not only in terms of individual books and individual projects, but I like to think that I'm in it for the long haul. It's the *doing* of it that gives me satisfaction. And that is what I try to keep my eye on. How I do it, whether it's writing a nonfiction book, or a poem, or interviewing somebody, or writing a novel, those are all parts of being a writer. You can't be a writer unless you are writing. I like the way Chester Himes put it: "A fighter fights, a writer writes."

There are many different stages of difficulty in writing for me that also depend upon what type of writing I am doing. With fiction sometimes the hardest work is the anxiety that I am never going to be able to do it. A fear that there's nothing there, that whatever I wrote last, good or bad, probably dried me up. I feel the same types of fears and anxieties as I did with my first book every time I start a new novel, only worse. Because when you're younger, you're more ignorant and innocent. One of the beauties of being young and just starting out is the ability to think, Well hell, *I'm* gonna do it! I really am Dostoyevsky, or Ralph Ellison in disguise! I'm definitely a swan! You know, you look like an ugly duckling, but you really do believe somewhere that you are a swan. Well, then you get to be thirty-five, and then you get to be fifty, and your neck still hasn't gotten real long, and you're not sliding so gracefully along the water's surface, and you realize that maybe you are not going to be a swan. So it becomes harder.

At the same time, I think I have a perspective on writing that I never had before. I am now sure that all that counts is pleasing myself. And I don't say that in an egotistical way, because in order to please myself, I have to really look closely at who I am and deal with the parts that make up myself. I am Betty Wideman's son, and I want her to be able to read my books. I have friends who write about fiction, friends who are writers themselves, from different countries and cultures. Toni Morrison and I, for instance, have through our books maintained a dialogue over the years about writing by virtue of the fact that the process continues and matures. I learn a lot from my students. So when I say that pleasing myself is all that counts, I mean that I am a representative of a broad range of feelings, interests, experiences, and I feel responsible to them all.

There are other angles and dimensions of writing that are very satisfying; if I can help someone, make them laugh or make them cry, teach them something about the world, or shed light on a problem—those are bonuses. But I can only do that if I am *thinking*, and if I am pleasing myself, enjoying the process, and using the writing to learn. The most pleasing part of the process is the actual putting down of the words on the page.

Writing requires a certain level of restraint. Because thinking is such an important part of the process, I don't want to be premature in putting down my thoughts. I don't mean holding back or censuring myself. Not that. I mean not writing on the particular project I am dealing with until I get something in my head that absolutely *demands* to come out. It has to feel right. It has to feel like the voice or the angle that I need. I depend on a sort of gestation period. What happens during it is partly unconcious, but since I have been doing it for so long, it is also partly conscious. I try to push myself to certain states of mind, to focus my energy, I listen to certain types of music, and so on.

Getting the words down on paper for the first time requires almost the opposite sort of push, because once the words start coming, I don't want to hold them back. Even when the words aren't fluid, or don't seem right, I keep writing. I may not know what I am writing, exactly where I am going along with a voice, or a character, or an idea; the project may be at the point where I still don't believe that it is going to be a book. It's still tentative. I don't know what shape the writing will actually take. I do know a lot of what I am writing is going to go right out the window. But at that point, I have to just keep plugging away, keep putting the words down.

Somewhere along in there, the material begins to become

more solid. I begin to have more confidence. I know the words better. The voices speak to me more clearly and more frequently. And then, I begin to reread and edit. I read the material over and over again, change maybe one word, or no words. When I get to the point of writing a final draft, I need to free myself, compress time, consume myself in the work because I am ready and anxious to have it finished. I write in longhand all the way through, so by the time the work gets to a final draft, I am also trying to get it ready for somebody else to transcribe it onto a computer.

I write in longhand because that's how I started writing, and I never learned to type. I also like the sensuous and tactile process—having the pen in my hand and looking at the letters flowing, and having the freedom to use different kinds of paper and different formats. Sometimes I think of the blank page as a canvas. The shape of the letters, their various slants, the color of the ink, and the texture of the paper—it's all part of the process.

Every book has its own story. Each book of mine has a different history of composition—how quickly it came, how much was conscious, how much was unconscious, and so on. There is no one way that I create or write. In talking with friends of mine who are also writers, I have discovered that every one has their own way of getting the words out, achieving what others may call a set style. Some writers have habits, some have learned their strengths and try to repeat what they have done before. But writing is an art, so it often does not respond to any kind of formula or preparation.

I do have different tendencies when I am writing nonfiction than when I am writing fiction. For instance, if I actually live through a scene, then some of the story is easier to re-create. But I think the scenes that are imagined can have just as much intensity as the ones that are based on an actual event because most actual events are a combination of different states of mind anyway. Like right now, sometimes I am focusing on the room and the things in it. I am very aware of you being here and asking me questions. And then at other times, depending upon the question you ask, I begin to go into my world, into my mind, to the cabin in Maine where I look out at the water and write. I think it is problematic where the mind of the writer is at any given moment. Realism is singular, when it should be plural.

When I lived in Wyoming, people used to ask me, "How the hell can you live in Wyoming and write about Pittsburgh? There are no black people around, and you write about black people?" I would respond by saying, for instance, if you were a woman in prison and you wanted to hold on to a relationship with a man outside of prison, you would have to work very hard at that relationship because you would not be able to touch that man. You may only see him very seldom, you may only hear his actual voice during those far-apart visits, so that you must try to remember what he sounds like the rest of the time. If you want that man to be present with you, you have to constantly work at imagining that he is there. If imagining is the only way that you can have him in your life, the work you do to keep him in your life is a sharpening and a heightening of your powers of imagination. Preserving the idea of him turns your imagination into a force for truth.

Any situation that I am in is something that I construct. It is not a given. If I had come to this interview after receiving word that a friend of mine had passed away, I would have a very different conversation. My state of mind would be completely different, and as soon as I walked through the door, I would have to decide how to play this situation, how to honor my feelings and at the same time pay attention to you. There is always interplay between the inside world and the outside world, and imagination works as both a mediator and an actively constructive element in any situation.

The difference between lying and imagining a situation has mostly to do with intention. The strategies are probably not all that different. I try to be up front about what my intentions are in my writing, and then somebody can judge me on those grounds rather than making me subject to rules or assumptions that are not mine. I try to set the rules of the game. No matter who sets the rules, there will always be ambiguities and gray areas, but if we are both on the same page, so to speak, then it is fair play. Lying has to do with making a very conscious attempt and effort to be on a different page, and to not be up front about your assumptions and intents, to trick someone, or to get something, or somewhere. It has to do with power.

I believe that life is existential, not essential. And that is the problem about race in this country—we really think that race exists. We think race tells us something essential, unchangeable, and absolute about people. When, in truth, race is a made-up idea that corresponds to a problematic reality. It is learned, it is taught, and it is conditioned. Nobody has proved any other source for race, no biological source anyway. That is not to say that culture and color are not real, because they are. Race is socially constructed in the way that bingo is socially constructed. I mean, people sat down and figured out this game they could play called bingo, and *then* it existed. But bingo is not a part of our biological inheritance, it does not have an essence that proves it has been here since the very beginning—it is a made-up game somebody invented. And in that sense, race is also a made-up thing. It was man-made for very particular reasons. It has a history. It is a concept that was invented to serve certain purposes—domination of one group by another—and it continues to serve its purposes. It maintains a very powerful hold on people's sense of identity.

To say that race doesn't exist will inevitably get people's hackles up, you know, folks will say, "Get that black son of a bitch to walk down *x* street in *x* town at *x* hour and then see if he thinks race doesn't exist!" But that's not what I am talking about. I'm talking about what is the significance of the concept, and how it operates as a word. It is not an essence located in human beings, it is a way of looking at human beings, manipulating and destroying human beings.

As I look back on my life, and think about my ancestors and my forebears, and the history of which I am a part, I try to include all of it in my writing. I try to include wisdom of my elders, and the situations in my life and in other people's lives that I think illustrate lessons and ask the right questions. Fiction is not about supplying answers, but rather about asking questions. So in my writing I try to raise problems: moving through one culture to another; being a person who has a foot in two worlds: reconciling groups and ideas in society that are most of the time hostile and at war with each other. If somebody reads my books and reads them seriously, I hope they may be acquiring some tools for asking useful questions about crucial issues.

I think that one of the toughest things to do is to not play to "the gallery." Or if you have to play to "the gallery," that is, if you have to become a sort of chameleon, that you retain some sort of control, some awareness of what color the chameleon actually is. I see young African-American people on the campus where I teach, and I think the kind of role playing that goes on is very dangerous if one is not grounded somewhere. Because one can get good at pretending and at playing someone else and then wake up one day and not be sure which identity is the real one. Which is a general problem for everybody in the twentieth century, but it is exacerbated if one is carrying the whole structure of race on one's shoulders. Because there are lots of other people dictating identities, and not only are they dictating, they have tremendous power to force us, trick us, into conforming.

I worry that certain elements of African-American culture are being destroyed and are being made to seem toxic so that they can be avoided. There is a class cleavage among black people, and always has been. America is a very class-ridden and -driven society. There is a real danger that black middle-class people may be in the front lines of the destruction of blacks in the lower economic segment. And that would be a disaster. Finding ways to prevent that sort of destruction from happening, on a very basic, intimate level, is what *Brothers and Keepers* is about. I saw myself and my own defection from family and community to get an education as somehow contributing to my brother's problem (life imprisonment). I didn't quite understand what was happening, and I'm not altogether clear now, but I'm more clear. I still wrestle with the issue, and as more black people become split by class, the problem refuses to go away. In *Brothers and Keepers*, I was talking of myself very much as an individual, a pioneer, but the social dynamics of the book can be applied today to larger groups. It's not a plot, it's not a scheme, it's not a conspiracy, but the politics of white domination alienate or cast out the poorest black people in our society. The black middle class participates in that alienation, becomes co-opted in various ways unless we consciously, systematically, resist. Some people relish the job of demonizing the black underclass, it seems, others are sort of squeamish, and some perhaps don't really understand what is happening.

There is a level at which self-awareness is crucial: I want to have at least some little idea of what I am doing and why I am doing it. I write notes to myself in a journal, which I have done for years and years. I do that simply to keep alive a place where I am thinking for myself, making my own decisions, where I am not making black decisions or mulatto decisions, just this little place where I can talk to myself without any interference. There have been times in my life when I have been very worried about losing access to that place. I depend on it. It's been my secret, a private corner, that private place where I think for myself.

I once thought I would like to write books that both my family in Pittsburgh and literary scholars could read and enjoy. Now I'd settle for writing books that just my family could read and enjoy. Because I know that any literary scholar who has good sense would also enjoy them. I think there is a universal ground serious readers can occupy, with room for many different kinds of writing and ideas. It's not black or white, rich or poor, educated or uneducated, it is something that is an amalgam; it's a blend that I would like to represent, speak to, and speak for.

The kind of writing I do requires participation. I'm not giving anything away. I am asking for your mind to meet my mind, and somewhere in the middle for the two of us to create something.

From
BROTHERS AND KEEPERS

Nothing changes. Nothing remains the same. One more visit to the prison, only this time, after I dropped my mother off at work, I tried a new route. The parkway had been undergoing repairs for two years. I'd used it anyway, in spite of detours and traffic jams. But this time I tried a shortcut my buddy Scott Payne had suggested. Scott was right; his way was quicker and freer of hassles. I'd arrived at Western Penitentiary in record time. Yet something was wrong. The new route transported me to the gates but I wasn't ready to pass through. Different streets, different buildings along the way hadn't done the trick, didn't have the power to take me where I needed to go because the journey to visit my brother in prison was not simply a matter of miles and minutes. Between Homewood and Woods Run, the flat, industrialized wasteland beside the river where the prison's hidden, there is a vast, uncharted space, a no-man's land where the traveler must begin to forget home and begin to remember the alien world inside "The Walls." At some point an invisible line is crossed, the rules change. Visitors must take leave of the certainties underpinning their everyday lives.

Using the parkway to reach Woods Run had become part of the ritual I depended upon to get me ready to see my brother. Huge green exit signs suspended over the highway, tires screaming on gouged patches of road surface, the darkness and claustrophobia of Squirrel Hill Tunnel, miles of abandoned steel-mill sheds, a mosque's golden cupola, paddle-wheeled pleasure boats moored at the riverbank, the scenes and sensations I catalogue now as I write were stepping stones. They broke the journey into stages, into moments I could anticipate. Paying attention to the steps allowed me to push into the back of my mind their inevitable destination, the place where the slide show of images was leading me.

I'd missed all that; so when I reached the last few miles of Ohio River Boulevard Scott's shortcut shared with my usual route, the shock of knowing the prison was just minutes away hit me harder than usual. I wasn't prepared to step through the looking glass.

Giving up one version of reality for another. That's what entering the prison was about. Not a dramatic flip-flop of values. That would be too easy. If black became white and good became bad and fast became slow, the players could learn the trick of reversing labels, and soon the upside-down world would seem natural. Prison is more perverse. Inside the walls nothing is certain, nothing can be taken for granted except the arbitrary exercise of absolute power. Rules engraved in stone one day will be superseded the next. What you don't know can always hurt you. And the prison rules are designed to keep you ignorant, keep you guessing, insure your vulnerability. Think of a fun-house mirror, a floor-to-ceiling sheet of undulating glass. Images ripple across its curved surface constantly changing. Anything caught in the mirror is bloated, distorted. Prison's like that mirror. Prison rules and regulations, the day-to-day operation of the institution, confront the inmate with an image of himself that is grotesque, absurd. A prisoner who refuses to internalize this image, who insists upon seeing other versions of himself, is in constant danger.

Somebody with a wry sense of humor had a field day naming the cluster of tiny streets bordering Western Penitentiary. Doerr, Refuge, Ketchum. When I reached the left turn at Doerr that would take me along the south wall of the prison to the parking-lot entrance, I still wasn't ready to go inside. I kept driving past the prison till the street I was on dead-ended. A U-turn in the lot of a chemical factory pointed me back toward the penitentiary and then for a few long minutes I sat in the car.

The city had vanished. Western Penitentiary was a million miles away. Taking a new route had been like reneging on my end of a bargain and now I had to pay the penalty. Certain magic words had not been chanted, the stone had not rolled away. I was displaced, out of time. Five days a week going about the business of earning a living, other people drove into the lot where I sat. Punching in and punching out. Doing their time in the shadow of the prison. The forty-foot-high stone walls did not exist for them. Caged men were a figment of someone's imagination, just as the workers parking in this lot each day were being imagined by me. How could one world reside so placidly next to the other? Men coming and going to their jobs, other men whose job was occupying the locked cells that created the prison. Ordinary men and prisoners, a factory and a penitentiary under the same gray sky. I couldn't move.

I heard myself in the factory cafeteria haranguing the workers:

Do you ever think about it? About that place over there? I mean when you drive by in the morning or when you're on your way home to your family or whatever? Do you see it? Do you ever wonder what's happening inside? What kind of men are locked up in there? Why are they inside and you outside? Can you imagine what happens when the lights go out at night? What do the prisoners think of you?

I'd lose my cool. Start shouting and pointing and get belligerent. People would be scared away. What kind of nut was I? Why was I hassling them? Go bug the prisoners. Preach to them. They're the bad guys.

Sitting alone in my mother's Chevette, the prison a half mile down the road, I turned off the motor so I could hear the factory humming and clanking within its low-slung brick walls behind my back. I was lost. The artificiality of *visiting* came down on me. I lived far away. Light-years away on a freezing planet, a planet empty except for the single solitary cell I inhabited. Visiting was illusion, deceit. I was separated from my brother by millions of stars. As distant as the employees of Chase Chemical Company who passed him every day on their way to work.

I focused on the ritual, the succession of things to be done in order to enter the prison. In my mind I passed through the iron gates of the official parking lot, I glanced at the stone walls, the river as I crossed the crowded lot to the visitors' annex. I climbed the steep concrete stairs. I faced the guard in his cage outside the waiting room, presented my identification, stated my brother's name and number, my relationship to him, wrote all that down on a sheet of mimeo paper, then found a seat in the dingy room, avoiding the blank faces of other visitors, frustration and anger building as I wait, wait, wait for the magic call that allows me down the steps, across a courtyard, up more steps, through steel doors and iron-barred doors into the lounge where my brother waits.

I saw it all happening, as it had happened many times before. Dreaming the process, the steps one by one, and then I could do it. Turn the key to start the engine. Begin the visit again.

During the half mile back down Preble Street I thought of death. Entertained the silly idea that what was most frightening about dying was the inability to rehearse it. You only died once, so you couldn't anticipate what would be required of you. You couldn't tame death by practicing. You couldn't ease it step by step from the darkness of the unknown into the light. Visiting prison is like going to a funeral parlor. Both situations demand unnatural responses, impose a peculiar discipline on the visitor. The need to hold on wars with the need to let go, and the visitor is stuck in the middle, doing both, doing neither. You are mourning, bereaved but you pretend the shell in the coffin is somehow connected with the vital, breathing person you once knew. You pretend a life has not been stolen, snatched away forever. You submit to the unnatural setting controlled by faceless intermediaries, even though you understand the setting has been contrived not so much to allay your grief, your sense of loss but to profit from them, mock them, and mock the one you need to see.

In the half mile back to the prison as the walls loom higher and nearer I asked the question I always must when a visit is imminent: Is Rob still alive? The possibility of sudden, violent death hangs over my brother's head every minute of every day so when I finally reach the guard's cage and ask for P3468, my heart stands still and I'm filled with the numbing irony of wishing, of praying that the guard will nod his head and say, Yes, your brother's still inside.

After the solid steel door, before the barred, locked gate into the visiting area proper, each visitor must pass through a metal-detecting machine. The reason for such a security measure is clear; the extreme sensitivity of the machine is less easily explained. Unless the point is inflicting humiliation on visitors. Especially women visitors whose underclothes contain metal stays and braces, women who wear intimate jewelry they never remove from their bodies. Grandmothers whose wedding rings are imbedded in the flesh of their fingers. When the machine bleeps, everything it discovers must go. You say it's a wire in your bra, lady. Well, I'm sorry about that but you gotta take it off. Of course the women have a choice. They can strip off the offending garment or ornament, and don one of the dowdy smocks the state provides for such contingencies. Or they can go back home.

I dump wallet, watch, change and belt in a plastic tray, kick off my sandals because they have metal buckles, tiptoe barefoot through the needle's eye without incident. I wonder about my kids' orthodonture. The next time they come to visit Robby, what will the machine say about the metal braces on their teeth? What will the guards say? Whose responsibility will it be to inspect the kids' mouths for weapons? Will the boys feel like horses on sale? Have I taught Dan and Jake enough about their history so that they'll recall auction blocks and professional appraisers of human flesh? And the silver chain Judy has worn since Jamila's birth? The good-luck charm she believes kept them both alive those terrible weeks in the hospital and hasn't left her neck since?

But I'm alone this trip and I pass through. No sweat. Not like the time in an airport during the early seventies when paranoia about skyjacking was rampant and a lone black male, youngish, large, athletically built, casually dressed, "fit" the profile of an air pirate and I was pulled aside for special searching. Who conceived the profile, who determined its accuracy, its scientific, objective utility, who decided it was okay to body-search an individual who fit the profile, were matters not discussed in public and certainly not with me. Protesting too vehemently either the search or its validity could quickly become a crime in itself. If not an offense serious enough to get you arrested, at least grounds for barring you from your flight. A question as highfalutin as the constitutionality of this hit-and-miss harassment, these kangeroo courts instantly set up in airports across the nation, such a question from a youngish, largish, casually dressed, lone, black male would have closed the case, proven the appropriateness of the profile for netting not only skyjackers but loudmouthed, radical militants.

As I passed through the prison's metal detector I was recalling my adventure in Denver's Stapleton airport and remembering another time around the Christmas holidays when my sons were forced to unload their new cowboy pistols from our carry-on bags and stow them in the baggage hold, a precaution I thought was silly, even funny, until I watched a passenger who arrived behind us talk his way onto the plane with a .38 in his briefcase. He was an off-duty cop, like the moonlighting security guards policing the baggage-inspection area. A whispered conversation, a couple hearty laughs and winks among good ole boys, a pat on the shoulder, and this white guy and his pistol were on the plane. Meanwhile my whole family was forced to wait for special cardboard containers that would secure my kids' toy guns out of reach in the plane's belly. Yes. I was angry both times. The stifled, gut-deep rage that's American as apple pie. The black rage that makes you want to strike out and smash somebody's face because you know they have you by the throat, killing you by inches. You know you're being singled out, discriminated against simply because the person doing it to you has the power to get away with it and you're powerless to stop him. Not funny when it happens. But in retrospect what could be more hilarious than a black American outraged because his rights are denied? Where's he been? Who's kidding whom? Hasn't the poor soul heard what Supreme Court Chief Justice Roger Taney announced loud and clear as the law of the land, a law lodged in the heart of the country, a law civil rights legislation has yet to unseat: Blacks "have no rights which the white man was bound to respect."

Rephrase Justice Taney's dictum so it reads, "The weak have no rights that the strong are bound to respect." Its universal applicability, its continuing force as law in the workings of our society becomes clear. Inscribe it in a slightly different form over the entrance to Western Penitentiary—*Prisoners have no rights that the keepers are bound to respect*—and you've generated the motto of the prison. Lots of words and much blood have been spilled attempting to justify, destroy, or sustain democratic institutions in America. An unresolved paradox remains always at the core of the notion of majority rule. Minority rights exist only at the sufferance of the majority, and since the majority is ultimately governed by self-interest, the majority's self-interest determines any minority's fate. No rights that they are bound to respect. Certainly not as long as they're bound to self-interest, to the greatest good for the greatest number. The keepers run prisons with little or no regard for prisoners' rights because license to exercise absolute power has been granted by those who rule society.

When a convicted criminal enters prison, he is first stripped of the clothing that connects him to the outside world. Re-dressed in a prison uniform, subjected to prison discipline, the inmate undergoes an abrupt transformation of who and what he is. The prisoner is being integrated into a new world, new terms of existence. Among orthodox Jews, a father may say Kaddish for a living son or daughter who has committed some unforgivable transgression. In this rare circumstance, Kaddish, a prayer of mourning, is also a declaration of death. The child becomes as dead to the father, a nonperson, cut off absolutely from all contact, a shadow the father will not acknowledge, a ghost referred to in the past tense as one who once was. Every day hundreds of prisoners experience a similar transition into a condition of nonexistence. Strangely, we have yet to name this declaration of civil death, this ritual that absolves us from responsibility for the prisoner's fate.

Although society declares to the prisoner you are no longer one of us, you are beyond the pale, the prisoner's body continues to breathe, his mind nags and races; he must be somewhere, something. He wants to know, as we all need to know: what am I? Into the vacuum society creates when it exiles the prisoner, step the keepers. In theory, their job is to guard incarcerated bodies, but because no one else speaks to the prisoners or for the prisoners, the keepers exercise an incredible power over their charges. Keepers can't pretend the inmates don't exist. They must create a landscape, an environment that secures the prisoners placed in their hands. As the keepers decide what time prisoners must awaken, when they may clean themselves, when they may eat, to whom they may speak, how they may wear their hair, which patches of ground they may march across and how long they may take crossing them, as the keepers constrict space and limit freedom, as the inmates are forced to conform to these mandates, an identity is fashioned for the prisoners. Guarding the inmates' bodies turns out to be a license for defining what a prisoner is. The tasks are complementary, in fact inseparable.

Prisoners are a unique minority; they exist in a political, ethical limbo via-à-vis free-world people. Out of sight, out of mind. Prisons segregate absolutely a troublesome minority from the majority. It's in the self-interest of the majority to suspend all ties to prisoners. A brutal but simple expedient for accomplishing this suspension is to lock up prisoners and charge the prisons with one task: keep these misfits away from us.

AUGUST

WILSON

AUGUST WILSON is the author of the plays *Ma Rainey's Black Bottom, Fences, Joe Turner's Come and Gone,* and *The Piano Lesson. Ma Rainey* opened on Broadway in October 1984 and won the New York Drama Critics' Circle Award. *Fences* opened on Broadway in March 1987 and won the Pulitzer Prize, the New York Drama Critics' Circle, the Drama Desk and Outer Critics' Circle awards, and a Tony Award. *Joe Turner* (1988) won the New York Drama Critics' Circle Award. *The Piano Lesson* (1990) won the Pulitzer Prize, the New York Drama Critics' Circle Award, and the Drama Desk Award. Wilson's most recent play, *Two Trains Running,* opened in 1990, and won the American Theater Critic Association Award and the New York Drama Critics' Circle Award. Wilson is also the recipient of a Guggenheim Fellowship and the Whiting Writer's Award. He is an alumnus of New Dramatists and a member of the American Academy of Arts and Sciences. He makes his home in Seattle, Washington, and is the proud father of daughter Sakina Ansari.

D URING THE SIXTIES, all of my friends were
painters, and when they were down and out and didn't
have no money, they'd be saying, "I need to get some
paint, man, 'cause I can't *say* what I need to *say* unless I get me
some yellow chrome, man. I ain't got no *yellow chrome*." I wanted
the tool that I would use to express myself with to *always* be available. So I chose a pen.

I first started writing poems for this girl in the seventh grade,
Nancy Ireland, who even the third graders were in love with. I
would leave the poems on her desk but would never sign my name
on any of them. Shortly after that, Nancy started going out with a
boy named Anthony Kerwin. I believe that he stole my poems and
told Nancy that he had written them. After that, I vowed the next
thing I wrote, no matter what it was, I would sign my name to it
and claim it as something that *I* had written.

My mother taught me and my five brothers and sisters how to
read. I remember going to school and passing the sign that read
HOSPITAL. I would just look at that word. It seemed as if the word
came alive, off of the sign and into the world. I also remember the
word *breakfast*, which I realized was actually *two* words making
one word. Then I think that was it, I was lost forever. After that, I
started to make up my own dictionary; I would take two and three
words, put them together, and then try to come up with my own
meaning for them.

By the time I got to writing those poems for Nancy Ireland, I
had already realized the power of writing. I had realized that I
could think of something and then concretize that thought on
paper with this prearrangement of symbols that each had their
own meaning. I could then go beyond what I was thinking and use

those same symbols to describe what I was feeling. Thinking and feeling became part of the same process.

I spent many years writing poetry. I once read that poetry is an enlargement of the say-able; it gives larger meaning to all of the things that we say, like "I don't know how to say that." Poetry describes all of the things that we cannot describe with the same old ordinary words by placing the same ordinary words in a different juxtaposition, applying certain words in a fresh way that will enable readers to see, feel, or to recognize something that is familiar to them. It is also a compressed way of speaking.

On the occasions when I used to read my poetry out loud, I would always start off with a poem that went like this:

> My face in the mirror
> the buttons on my coat
> the coin in my pocket.
> These are my compatriots.
> My compatriots and I ask for your attention.
> We are going to begin now.

It gives the idea of saying a lot in a very small amount of space, and a commitment has been made to a certain idea. I think poetry is the most difficult medium to write in. John Berryman has two lines which to me capture the essence of what poetry is: *I saw nobody coming,/So I went instead*. Poetry is the distillation of language; the words are boiled down into their purest form. In poetry, you can make a few words do a lot of work.

My experience with writing short fiction has allowed me to fill in all the spaces that must be left unfilled in drama. With playwriting, I have to make the dialogue of the characters do so much.

Whereas with fiction, I can write everything and describe the way a character actually feels, or the way something is said or seen. In fiction, all of the information needs to be supplied for the reader to decipher. In drama, the actor brings all of that information when he embodies the text and walks out onstage; the audience member is given the information from the way the character looks and so forth without necessarily participating.

The audience in a theater gives the sense of a community experience while sharing the singular event of a play. The act of someone sitting on a bus and reading a book is a solitary act. Wherever you read—in bed, in the bathroom, on the porch—you are still alone. In theater, you and five hundred other people are going to witness the same thing. If an actor comes out and stumbles on his way to the stage, then that becomes part of the performance, and everyone in the audience, as well as onstage, will experience it.

I am aware of the craft of playwriting in the sense that I have to manipulate the material in such a way that it will keep the audience interested and informed about what is going on. I don't write for any particular audience, but the idea of audience is built into the craft of playwriting. In terms of what that audience may specifically look like, it looks like me. I have to satisfy the audience that is myself. I don't write for a black or white audience beyond that.

I sort of stumbled into playwriting. I wrote a series of poems about a black character that was probably, although not intentionally, based loosely on one of Ishmael Reed's poems, when he wrote poetry—"The Ballad of the Bad Man Professor," or something like that. Anyway, this character that I created was called Black Bart, and he was an alchemist magician. Black Bart carved out this retreat called The Sacred Hills, which was protected by electric invisible angels. You could only get into this retreat if you had a pure heart. Bart lived behind that screen of electric angels and did a lot of pontificating about the world outside. A friend of mine heard me read one time and told me that I should turn the poems into a play. I said to him, "Come on, man, get serious, it's just a poem." But my friend was persistent, and so the seed was planted.

Me and my friend gathered a few other friends and we all got together for maybe four weekends in a row to talk about making my poems into a play. And then I started thinking that I didn't want anyone else to write *my play*, so I stayed home from one Sunday to the next and wrote it myself. I extended the idea of Black Bart and turned it into a satire on American society.

I discovered the Negro section of the Carnegie Library when I was fourteen years old and on my way home from playing basketball. There were about thirty books in that section. This began my growing awareness of being black. I remember coming across some kind of obscure sociological textbook in that section about the Negro's power of hard work. At the time, there was a blind man who I knew named Mister Douglass, and I used to cut his lawn. I remember feeling very proud that a blind man let me cut his lawn, because it meant that he trusted that I would do a good job. After I read that textbook, I don't think I cut that man's lawn so much as I *plowed* it. I mean, I went out there just ready to take on the world! And it was because of that strange book that discussed the Negro's power of hard work. I had never encountered the words *Negro* and *power* in the same sentence before. Little did I know that those two words would later became a movement: Black Power.

I began to identify positions of authority when I was about seven years old—the landlord, the bus driver, the storekeeper, the schoolteacher, the clerk at the welfare office. I recognized immediately that they were all white. So my relationship with society was dictated in my mind at that early point in my life. And after I discovered the Negro section in the library, and read those thirty or so books, I began to understand why.

Where I lived, me and my friends had to get each other together before we went anywhere. My mom would tell me to go to the A&P, and I'd go over to Cole's house first and say, "Yo man, I gots to go down to Second Street, man, to the A&P," and he'd say, "Awright, let's get Jesse then, come on." It was like that because the white people around our neighborhood would throw rocks at our windows and yell "Nigger!" at us as they drove by. We each carried our own stick. It was funny because one day, we were looking at the TV and there was this show on about Africans, and they were carrying sticks! I told the guys, "Hey look, man, that's us!" We hadn't ever known why we carried our sticks, it was just the way it was.

In 1965, I lived on Fifth Avenue in Pittsburgh, across the street from the St. Vincent de Paul Store. I was very poor, and I couldn't afford to buy any record albums, but I loved music. The St. Vincent de Paul Store sold 78's for a nickel apiece. So I bought one, along with a three-dollar record player that played 78's. Nobody else wanted it because nobody else was buying 78's, just 45's then. So I took it home and put the record on. It was Patti Page, who was very popular at the time. Well, I kept buying those nickel 78's, bringing them home and listening to them. Occasionally I would run into an Ella Fitzgerald, or maybe a Coleman Hawkins, but mainly just Patti Page. I bought the records indiscriminately, just to hear music.

One day I came across a record called *Nobody in Town Could Make a Sweet Jelly Roll Like Mine* by someone named Bessie Smith. I put that record on, and I'll tell you, I felt as though she was talking directly to me. The universe stuttered when I heard her voice. I played it again, and again, over and over. The world

began to change in front of my eyes. The other records disappeared. The people around me suddenly began to look different;
the counterfeiter in my rooming house downstairs who would try
to get me into his trouble, the landlady who was always battling
with the tenants upstairs and always threatening to kill herself, you
know, I looked at them all differently. It's hard to articulate the
awareness I felt after hearing that record. I went over to St. Vincent de Paul the next morning to try and find another Bessie
Smith record.

The sound of Bessie Smith's voice represented something else
in the world that I needed to find out about. She was a link, in the
same way that discovering the Negro section in the library was a
link—to the richness of black culture. I went from Bessie Smith to
Malcolm X.

My good friend in Pittsburgh, Black Black Rob—he was so
black, we had to say it twice—he was all about the Negritude
Poets, and he'd always have a stack of Malcolm X records under
his arm. People would see him coming and would say, "Aw, here
comes Rob with that black stuff!" Rob was always turning me on
to new ideas. At that time, without ever having really looked into
it, I thought Malcolm was this evil, weird persona preaching violence. So one time Rob told me to come and listen to some of
these Malcom X records that he had. We went over to Clarence
Jones's house and listened to those records. That changed my
world.

After that, Rob and I started a theater that was very political
and righteous. It was the middle of the Black Power movement,
and I felt it was an honor and a duty to constantly search for ways
to alter my relationship to society. We hoped that the type of per-
formances we produced at our theater would raise the consciousness of people, and in doing so, we realized ourselves how

powerful theater could be. That led me to the first real instance of using theater as a medium for communication. By this time, I had the ball in my arm and was running for the end zone, you know—I had the ball in my arm. Of course I got tackled a few times along the way, but at least I knew where the end zone was.

I got all the way through the Black Power movement, when everyone was a revolutionary or a radical poet, without having my writing be about politics. People let me read my poetry and accepted it for what it was because I ran the theater where everyone else was reading. I never felt that art was about politics. I remember guys walking around with John Coltrane records. I couldn't get into jazz because it didn't have any words. I was more interested in following the tradition of folklore. I got up to read at a poetry reading one time. I had written a poem about trains, because trains are a very important part of all of our lives; most folks had come up north on the train and what have you. So I got up there and started talking about trains. Well, the place erupted. They thought I was talking about "Trane" as in Col-Trane. Once I got into the poem and people understood that I was actually talking about trains, not John Coltrane, the audience died down.

Now I feel that my writing *is* very political. It has taken me many years to accomplish that, to be able to bridge that gap. The turning point was really when I started writing plays as opposed to just producing them and was able to carve out a specific territory for myself. I was responding to James Baldwin's call in one of his essays when he asked for "a profound articulation of the Black Tradition," which he defined as "the ritual of intercourse that can sustain a man once he leaves his father's house." And I thought, Well, yeah, that's what I'm doing! That's what my writing has always been about. But I didn't know that it was political until I realized that I was responding to a call, which is inherently politi-

cal action. My writing is rooted in the blues, and it is a demonstra-
tion of black culture's existence as well as its capacity to offer sus-
tenance.

One difficult transition in my writing was learning how to
respect and gain a true sense of the value of black language as it is
spoken. For the longest time I couldn't make my characters talk. I
thought in order to incorporate the black vernacular into literature, the language had to be changed or altered in some way to
sound more clear. I wrote this play once about an old man and an
old woman on a park bench. In the first line of the play the old
man looks at the old woman and says, "Our lives are frozen in the
deepest cold and spiritual turbulence." She just looks at him.
"Terror hangs over the night like a hawk. Your black skin trembles
in the cold." And he goes on with all of this sort of metaphorical,
romantic prose language. That is the kind of writing I was doing
for a long time until I realized that it was no less romantic and
meaningful to say, "It's cold outside." And again, I was able to
understand that to some extent through music.

When I decided to write, I said to myself, Now, if you're going
to do this, then you're going to have to be honest. I knew that I
couldn't just pick out the good parts, I had to go all the way. And I
had to get a feel for the cultural response to the world and the
social battles of black America. All I had to do was to pick up a
record of blues music—which will tell anyone all that they need to
know about black people in America—and I was able to re-create
our people through writing, our ideas of social conduct, our sym-
metry and grace, pleasure and pain.

From

FENCES

Act One, Scene Three

The lights come up on the yard. It is four hours later. ROSE is taking down the clothes from the line. CORY enters carrying his football equipment.

ROSE: Your daddy like to had a fit with you running out of here this morning without doing your chores.

CORY: I told you I had to go to practice.

ROSE: He say you were supposed to help him with this fence.

CORY: He been saying that the last four or five Saturdays, and then he don't never do nothing, but go down to Taylors'. Did you tell him about the recruiter?

ROSE: Yeah, I told him.

CORY: What he say?

ROSE: He ain't said nothing too much. You get in there and get started on your chores before he gets back. Go on and scrub down them steps before he gets back here hollering and carrying on.

CORY: I'm hungry. What you got to eat, Mama?

ROSE: Go on and get started on your chores. I got some meat loaf in there. Go on and make you a sandwich . . . and don't leave no mess in there.

(CORY exits into the house. ROSE continues to take down the clothes. TROY enters the yard and sneaks up and grabs her from behind.)

Troy! Go on, now. You liked to scared me to death. What was the score of the game? Lucille had me on the phone and I couldn't keep up with it.

TROY: What I care about the game? Come here, woman. (*He tries to kiss her.*)

ROSE: I thought you went down Taylors' to listen to the game. Go on, Troy! You supposed to be putting up this fence.

TROY: (*Attempting to kiss her again.*) I'll put it up when I finish with what is at hand.

ROSE: Go on, Troy. I ain't studying you.

TROY: (*Chasing after her.*) I'm studying you . . . fixing to do my homework!

ROSE: Troy, you better leave me alone.

TROY: Where's Cory? That boy brought his butt home yet?

ROSE: He's in the house doing his chores.

TROY: (*Calling.*) Cory! Get your butt out here, boy!

(*ROSE exits into the house with the laundry. TROY goes over to the pile of wood, picks up a board, and starts sawing. CORY enters from the house.*)

TROY: You just now coming in here from leaving this morning?

CORY: Yeah, I had to go to football practice.

TROY: Yeah, what?

CORY: Yessir.

TROY: I ain't but two seconds off you noway. The garbage sitting in there overflowing . . . you ain't done none of your chores . . . and you come in here talking about "Yeah."

CORY: I was just getting ready to do my chores now, Pop . . .

TROY: Your first chore is to help me with this fence on Saturday. Everything else come after that. Now get that saw and cut them boards.

(CORY takes the saw and begins cutting the boards. TROY continues working. There is a long pause.)

CORY: Hey, Pop . . . why don't you buy a TV?

TROY: What I want with a TV? What I want one of them for?

CORY: Everybody got one. Earl, Ba Bra . . . Jesse!

TROY: I ain't asked you who had one. I say what I want with one?

CORY: So you can watch it. They got lots of things on TV. Baseball games and everything. We could watch the World Series.

TROY: Yeah . . . and how much this TV cost?

CORY: I don't know. They got them on sale for around two hundred dollars.

TROY: Two hundred dollars, huh?

CORY: That ain't that much, Pop.

TROY: Naw, it's just two hundred dollars. See that roof you got over your head at night? Let me tell you something about that roof. It's been over ten years since that roof was last tarred. See now . . . the snow come this winter and sit up there on that roof like it is . . . and it's gonna seep inside. It's just gonna be a little bit

. . . ain't gonna hardly notice it. Then the next thing you know, it's gonna be leaking all over the house. Then the wood rot from all that water and you gonna need a whole new roof. Now, how much you think it cost to get that roof tarred?

CORY: I don't know.

TROY: Two hundred and sixty-four dollars . . . cash money. While you thinking about a TV, I got to be thinking about the roof . . . and whatever else go wrong around here. Now if you had two hundred dollars, what would you do . . . fix the roof or buy a TV?

CORY: I'd buy a TV. Then when the roof started to leak . . . when it needed fixing . . . I'd fix it.

TROY: Where you gonna get the money from? You done spent it for a TV. You gonna sit up and watch the water run all over your brand new TV.

CORY: Aw, Pop. You got money. I know you do.

TROY: Where I got it at, huh?

CORY: You got it in the bank.

TROY: You wanna see my bankbook? You wanna see that seventy-three dollars and twenty-two cents I got sitting up in there?

CORY: You ain't got to pay for it all at one time. You can put a down payment on it and carry it on home with you.

TROY: Not me. I ain't gonna owe nobody nothing if I can help it. Miss a payment and they come and snatch it right out your house. Then what you got? Now, soon as I get two hundred dollars clear, then I'll buy a TV. Right now, as soon as I get two hundred and sixty-four dollars, I'm gonna have this roof tarred.

CORY: Aw . . . Pop!

TROY: You go on and get you two hundred dollars and buy one if ya want it. I got better things to do with my money.

CORY: I can't get no two hundred dollars. I ain't never seen two hundred dollars.

TROY: I'll tell you what . . . you get you a hundred dollars and I'll put the other hundred with it.

CORY: Alright, I'm gonna show you.

TROY: You gonna show me how you can cut them boards right now.

(CORY begins to cut the boards. There is a long pause.)

CORY: The Pirates won today. That makes five in a row.

TROY: I ain't thinking about the Pirates. Got an all-white team. Got that boy . . . that Puerto Rican boy . . . Clemente. Don't even half-play him. That boy could be something if they give him a chance. Play him one day and sit him on the bench the next.

CORY: He gets a lot of chances to play.

TROY: I'm talking about playing regular. Playing every day so you can get your timing. That's what I'm talking about.

CORY: They got some white guys on the team that don't play every day. You can't play everybody at the same time.

TROY: If they got a white fellow sitting on the bench . . . you can bet your last dollar he can't play! The colored guy got to be twice as good before he get on the team. That's why I don't want you to get all tied up in them sports. Man on the team and what it get him? They got colored on the team and don't use them. Same as not having them. All them teams the same.

CORY: The Braves got Hank Aaron and Wes Covington. Hank Aaron hit two home runs today. That makes forty-three.

TROY: Hank Aaron ain't nobody. That's what you supposed to do. That's how you supposed to play the game. Ain't nothing to it. It's just a matter of timing . . . getting the right follow-through. Hell, I can hit forty-three home runs right now!

CORY: Not off no major-league pitching, you couldn't.

TROY: We had better pitching in the Negro leagues. I hit seven home runs off of Satchel Paige. You can't get no better than that!

CORY: Sandy Koufax. He's leading the league in strikeouts.

TROY: I ain't thinking of no Sandy Koufax.

CORY: You got Warren Spahn and Lew Burdette. I bet you couldn't hit no home runs off of Warren Spahn.

TROY: I'm through with it now. You go on and cut them boards.

(*Pause.*)

Your mama tell me you done got recruited by a college football team? Is that right?

CORY: Yeah. Coach Zellman say the recruiter gonna be coming by to talk to you. Get you to sign the permission papers.

TROY: I thought you supposed to be working down there at the A&P. Ain't you suppose to be working down there after school?

CORY: Mr. Stawicki say he gonna hold my job for me until after the football season. Say starting next week I can work weekends.

TROY: I thought we had an understanding about this football stuff? You suppose to keep up with your chores and hold that job down at the A&P. Ain't been around here all day on a Saturday. Ain't none of your chores done . . . and now you telling me you done quit your job.

CORY: I'm gonna be working weekends.

TROY: You damn right you are! And ain't no need for nobody coming around here to talk to me about signing nothing.

CORY: Hey, Pop . . . you can't do that. He's coming all the way from North Carolina.

TROY: I don't care where he coming from. The white man ain't gonna let you get nowhere with that football noway. You go on and get your book-learning so you can work yourself up in that A&P or learn how to fix cars or build houses or something, get you a trade. That way you have something can't nobody take away from you. You go on and learn how to put your hands to some good use. Besides hauling people's garbage.

CORY: I get good grades, Pop. That's why the recruiter wants to talk with you. You got to keep up your grades to get recruited. This way I'll be going to college. I'll get a chance . . .

TROY: First you gonna get your butt down there to the A&P and get your job back.

CORY: Mr. Stawicki done already hired somebody else 'cause I told him I was playing football.

TROY: You a bigger fool than I thought . . . to let somebody take away your job so you can play some football. Where you gonna get your money to take out your girlfriend and whatnot? What kind of foolishness is that to let somebody take away your job?

CORY: I'm still gonna be working weekends.

TROY: Naw . . . naw. You getting your butt out of here and finding you another job.

CORY: Come on, Pop! I got to practice. I can't work after school and play football too. The team needs me. That's what Coach Zellman say . . .

TROY: I don't care what nobody else say. I'm the boss . . . you understand? I'm the boss around here. I do the only saying what counts.

CORY: Come on, Pop!

TROY: I asked you . . . did you understand?

CORY: Yeah . . .

TROY: What?!

CORY: Yessir.

TROY: You go on down there to that A&P and see if you can get your job back. If you can't do both . . . then you quit the football team. You've got to take the crookeds with the straights.

CORY: Yessir.

(*Pause.*)

Can I ask you a question?

TROY: What the hell you wanna ask me? Mr. Stawicki the one you got the questions for.

CORY: How come you ain't never liked me?

TROY: Liked you? Who the hell say I got to like you? What law is there say I got to like you? Wanna stand up in my face and ask a damn fool-ass question like that. Talking about liking somebody. Come here, boy, when I talk to you.

(CORY comes over to where TROY is working. He stands slouched over and TROY shoves him on his shoulder.)

Straighten up, goddammit! I asked you a question . . . what law is there say I got to like you?

CORY: None.

TROY: Well, alright then! Don't you eat every day?

(Pause.)

Answer me when I talk to you ! Don't you eat every day?

CORY: Yeah.

TROY: Nigger, as long as you in my house, you put that sir on the end of it when you talk to me!

CORY: Yes . . . sir.

TROY: You eat every day.

CORY: Yessir!

TROY: Got a roof over your head.

CORY: Yessir!

TROY: Got clothes on your back.

CORY: Yessir.

TROY: Why you think that is?

CORY: 'Cause of you.

TROY: Aw, hell I know it's 'cause of me . . . but why do you think that is?

CORY: (*Hesitant.*) 'Cause you like me.

TROY: Like you? I go out of here every morning . . . bust my butt . . . putting up with them crackers every day . . . 'cause I like you? You about the biggest fool I ever saw.

(*Pause.*)

It's my job. It's my responsibility! You understand that? A man got to take care of his family. You live in my house . . . sleep you behind on my bedclothes . . . fill you belly up with my food . . . 'cause you my son. You my flesh and blood. Not 'cause I like you! 'Cause it's my duty to take care of you. I owe a responsibility to you! Let's get this straight right here . . . before it go along any further . . . I ain't got to like you. Mr. Rand don't give me my money come payday 'cause he likes me. He gives me 'cause he owe me. I done give you everything I had to give you. I gave you your life! Me and your mama worked that out between us. And liking your black ass wasn't part of the bargain. Don't you try and go through life worrying about if somebody like you or not. You best be making sure they doing right by you. You understand what I'm saying, boy?

CORY: Yessir.

TROY: Then get the hell out of my face, and get on down to that A&P.

(ROSE has been standing behind the screen door for much of the scene. She enters as CORY exits.)

ROSE: Why don't you let the boy go ahead and play football, Troy? Ain't no harm in that. He's just trying to be like you with the sports.

TROY: I don't want him to be like me! I want him to move as far away from my life as he can get. You the only decent thing that ever happened to me. I wish him that. But I don't wish him a thing else from my life. I decided seventeen years ago that boy wasn't getting involved in no sports. Not after what they did to me in the sports.

ROSE: Troy, why don't you admit you was too old to play in the major leagues? For once . . . why don't you admit that?

TROY: What do you mean too old? Don't come telling me I was too old. I just wasn't the right color. Hell, I'm fifty-three years old and can do better than Selkirk's .269 right now!

ROSE: How's was you gonna play ball when you were over forty? Sometimes I can't get no sense out of you.

TROY: I got good sense, woman. I got sense enough not to let my boy get hurt over playing no sports. You been mothering that boy too much. Worried about if people like him.

ROSE: Everything that boy do . . . he do for you. He wants you to say "Good job, son." That's all.

TROY: Rose, I ain't got time for that. He's alive. He's healthy. He's got to make his own way. I made mine. Ain't nobody gonna hold his hand when he get out there in that world.

ROSE: Times have changed from when you was young, Troy. People change. The world's changing around you and you can't even see it.

TROY: (*Slow, methodical.*) Woman . . . I do the best I can do. I come in here every Friday. I carry a sack of potatoes and a bucket of lard. You all line up at the door with your hands out. I give you the lint from my pockets. I give you my sweat and my blood. I ain't got no tears. I done spent them. We go upstairs in that room at night . . . and I fall down on you and try to blast a hole into forever. I get up Monday morning . . . find my lunch on the table. I go out. Make my way. Find my strength to carry me through to the next Friday.

(*Pause.*)

That's all I got, Rose. That's all I got to give. I can't give nothing else.

(*TROY exits into the house. The lights go down to black.*)